Just Spring

Madhusudhan Konda

O'REILLY®

Beijing · Cambridge · Farnham · Köln · Sebastopol · Tokyo

Just Spring

by Madhusudhan Konda

Printed in the United States of America.

Published by O'Reilly Media, Inc., 1005 Gravenstein Highway North, Sebastopol, CA 95472.

O'Reilly books may be purchased for educational, business, or sales promotional use. Online editions are also available for most titles (*http://my.safaribooksonline.com*). For more information, contact our corporate/institutional sales department: (800) 998-9938 or *corporate@oreilly.com*.

Editors: Meghan Blanchette and Mike Loukides	**Cover Designer:** Randy Comer
Production Editor: Christopher Hearse	**Interior Designer:** David Futato
Copyeditor: Nan Reinhardt	**Illustrator:** Rebecca Demarest

July 2011:   First Edition

Revision History for the First Edition:

2011-09-23:   First release

2013-02-28:   Second release

See *http://oreilly.com/catalog/errata.csp?isbn=9781449306403* for release details.

ISBN: 978-1-449-30640-3

[LSI]

Table of Contents

Preface

The Spring Framework is very mature. It has been embraced by the industry and attracted a strong user base. It is challenging to write on a subject that has already been inundated with so many books, manuals, articles, and tutorials, including videos.

So, what is my motivation for writing this book?

I have come in contact with many programmers and developers who sometimes stumble on the basics. They often feel shy about asking colleagues for help. I have also met a few who have had no prior Spring experience before being pushed onto Spring projects. They were given no training or guidance, but were expected to contribute overnight. There's a third group of people who are genuinely interested in learning Spring but may be put off by the big texts or manuals. These people are enthusiastic and want to hit the ground running, but they don't have the time or patience to read and digest volumes of data! They only have time to read a simple book, understand the technology, and jump straight into practice. Once they get a hang of it, their grey matter will ask for more and more.

When I want to learn something new, I like to start with basics (I may lean toward the last category), experiment with code, move an inch further, burn a bit of code, and so on. Once I "feel" the technology, then I wish to quench my thirst. At that point, I seek out the advanced, in-depth manuals and specs, and of course, the big books.

This is my motive behind the *Just Spring* series of books. Simple yet powerful.

My aim is to deliver simple, straight-to-the-point, no nonsense, and example-driven books on Spring projects. And of course, I'd like them to be page-turners and easy reads.

These books should give you enough knowledge and confidence to start working on the real-world projects.

The current book covers the backbone of Spring—the core (it will be renamed *Just Spring Core* soon). If you are interested in learning nothing but Spring, then *Just Spring* is your companion. If you wish to get introduced to Spring quickly and precisely, or would like to refresh your knowledge on Spring in couple of hours, or have only a weekend to learn Spring before you start working on it on Monday, this is the book that you should choose. It does not cover any other Spring subjects such as Spring MVC or Spring Integration. They are covered by different books in the *Just Spring* series.

I sincerely thank you all for embracing this book. I have received positive feedback, reviews, comments, suggestions, and praises that have certainly encouraged me to do more. I hope you have all enjoyed it as much as I have writing it! Please get in touch with me, even if you are unhappy with me or my writings.

Other *Just Spring* books are on their way! Stay tuned.

Madhusudhan Konda

www.madhusudhan.com (*http://www.madhusudhan.com*)

On Twitter *@mkonda007*

Conventions Used in This Book

The following typographical conventions are used in this book:

Italic

> Indicates new terms, URLs, email addresses, filenames, and file extensions.

`Constant width`

> Used for program listings, as well as within paragraphs to refer to program elements such as variable or function names, databases, data types, environment variables, statements, and keywords.

`Constant width bold`

> Shows commands or other text that should be typed literally by the user.

`Constant width italic`

> Shows text that should be replaced with user-supplied values or by values determined by context.

Using Code Examples

This book is here to help you get your job done. In general, you may use the code in this book in your programs and documentation. You do not need to contact us for permission unless you're reproducing a significant portion of the code. For example, writing a program that uses several chunks of code from this book does not require permission. Selling or distributing a CD-ROM of examples from O'Reilly books does require permission. Answering a question by citing this book and quoting example code does not require permission. Incorporating a significant amount of example code from this book into your product's documentation does require permission.

We appreciate, but do not require, attribution. An attribution usually includes the title, author, publisher, and ISBN. For example: "*Just Spring* by Madhusudhan Konda (O'Reilly). Copyright 2013 Madhusudhan Konda, 978-1-449-30640-3."

If you feel your use of code examples falls outside fair use or the permission given here, feel free to contact us at *permissions@oreilly.com*.

You can download this book's code examples here:

http://examples.oreilly.com/0636920020394/

Safari® Books Online

 Safari Books Online is an on-demand digital library that lets you easily search over 7,500 technology and creative reference books and videos to find the answers you need quickly.

With a subscription, you can read any page and watch any video from our library online. Read books on your cell phone and mobile devices. Access new titles before they are available for print, and get exclusive access to manuscripts in development and post feedback for the authors. Copy and paste code samples, organize your favorites, download chapters, bookmark key sections, create notes, print out pages, and benefit from tons of other time-saving features.

O'Reilly Media has uploaded this book to the Safari Books Online service. To have full digital access to this book and others on similar topics from O'Reilly and other publishers, sign up for free at *http://my.safaribooksonline.com*.

How to Contact Us

Please address comments and questions concerning this book to the publisher:

O'Reilly Media, Inc.
1005 Gravenstein Highway North
Sebastopol, CA 95472
800-998-9938 (in the United States or Canada)
707-829-0515 (international or local)
707-829-0104 (fax)

We have a web page for this book, where we list errata, examples, and any additional information. You can access this page at: *http://oreil.ly/just-spring*

To comment or ask technical questions about this book, send email to:

bookquestions@oreilly.com

For more information about our books, courses, conferences, and news, see our website at *http://www.oreilly.com*.

Find us on Facebook: *http://facebook.com/oreilly*

Follow us on Twitter: *http://twitter.com/oreillymedia*

Watch us on YouTube: *http://www.youtube.com/oreillymedia*

Content Updates

September 23, 2011

- Added the following sections to Chapter 2:
  - — "Using Annotations"
  - — "XML Namespaces"
- Updated source code.
- Added an introduction to Preface.

February 28, 2013

- Revised and improved all chapters; some sections were rewritten.
- Enhanced codebase.
- Especially improved content of Chapter 5, *Spring JMS* and Chapter 6, *Spring Data*.

Acknowledgments

I sincerely wish to thank my editor, Mike Loukides, for keeping faith in me and directing me when lost. Also to all of those in the O'Reilly team, especially Meghan Blanchette, Holly Bauer, Sarah Schneider, Christopher Hearse, and Dan Fauxsmith, for helping shape this book

Sincere thanks to my loving wife, Jeannette, for being very patient and supportive throughout the writing of this book. Also to my wonderful six-year-old son, Joshua, who surprisingly sacrificed his free time, allowing me to write when I explained to him what I was doing!

I also thank my family in India for their wonderful support and love.

In memory of my loving Dad!

CHAPTER 1

Basics

Introduction

The Spring Framework has found a very strong user base over the years. Software houses and enterprises found the framework to be the best fit for their plumbing needs. Surprisingly, the core principle that Spring has been built for—the *Dependency Injection* (DI)—is very simple and straightforward to understand. In this chapter, we aim to discusses the fundamentals of the framework from a high ground. We will try to get a basic understanding of Dependency Injection principles. I will present a simple problem of object coupling and tight dependencies to begin with. Then we will aim to solve decoupling and dependencies by using Spring Framework.

Object Coupling Problem

Let us consider a simple program whose aim is to read data from various data sources. It should read data from a file system or database or even from an FTP server.

For simplicity, we will start writing a program that reads the data from a file system. The following example code is written *without* employing any best practices or dependency injection patterns—it's just a simple and plain Java program that works.

This snippet shows a `VanillaDataReaderClient` class that uses `FileReader` to fetch the data.

Example 1-1.

```
public class VanillaDataReaderClient {
  private FileReader fileReader = null;
  private String fileName = "src/main/resources/basics/basics-trades-data.txt";

  public VanillaDataReaderClient() {
    try {
      fileReader = new FileReader(fileName);
```

```
    } catch (FileNotFoundException e) {
      System.out.println("Exception" + e.getMessage());
    }
  }

  private String fetchData() {
    return fileReader.read();
  }

  public static void main(String[] args) {
    VanillaDataReaderClient dataReader = new VanillaDataReaderClient();
    System.out.println("Got data using no-spring: " + dataReader.fetchData());
  }
}
```

As the name suggests, the VanillaDataReaderClient is the client that fetches the data from a data source. When the program is executed, the VanillaDataReaderClient gets instantiated along with a referenced FileReader object. It then uses the Vanilla FileReader object to fetch the result.

The following snippet shows the implementation of VanillaFileReader class:

Example 1-2.

```
public class VanillaFileReader {
  private StringBuilder builder = null;
  private Scanner scanner = null;

  public VanillaFileReader(String fileName) throws FileNotFoundException {
    scanner = new Scanner(new File(fileName));
    builder = new StringBuilder();
  }

  public String read() {
    while (scanner.hasNext()) {
      builder.append(scanner.next());
      builder.append(",");
    }
    return builder.toString();
  }
}
```

Simple and sweet, isn't it?

The limitation of the client above is that it can *only* read the data from file system.

Imagine, one fine morning, your manager asks you to improvise the program to read data from a Database or Socket instead of File.

With the current design, it is not possible to incorporate these changes without refac-toring the code—as only File Reader associated to the client, it can't work for any non-file resources. We have to associate a *DatabaseReader* or *SocketReader* with the client for any non-file resource reading excercise.

Lastly (and very importantly), we can see the client and the reader are coupled tightly. That is, client depends on `VanillaFileReader`'s contract, meaning if `VanillaFileReader` changes, so does the client. If the client has already been distributed and used by, say, 1,000 users across the globe, you will have fun refactoring the client!

If your intention is to build good scalable and testable components, then coupling is a bad thing.

So, let's work out on your manager's demands and make the program read the data from any source. For this, we will take this program one step further—refactoring so the client can read from any datasource. For this refactoring, we have to rely on our famous *Design to Interfaces* principle.

Designing to Interfaces

Writing your code against interfaces is a very good practice, although I am not going to sing praises about the best practices of designing here. The first step in designing to interfaces is to create an interface. The concrete classes will implement this interface, binding themselves to the interface contract rather than to an implementation. As long as you keep the interface contract unchanged, the implementation can be modified any number of times without affecting the client.

For our data reader program, we create an `IReader` interface. This has just one method:

```
public interface IReader {
  public String read();
}
```

The next step is to implement this contract. Because we have to read the data from different sources, we create respective concrete implementations such as `FileReader` for reading from a File System, `DatabaseReader` for reading from a Database, `FtpReader` for reading from FTP Server, and so on.

The template for concrete implementation goes in the form of *XXXReader* as shown here:

```
public class XXXReader implements IReader {
  public String read(){
    //impl goes here
  }
}
```

Once you have the `XXXReader` ready, the next step is to use it in the client program. However, instead of using the concrete class reference, we will be using the interface reference.

For example, the modified client program shown in this snippet has a IReader variable reference (highlighted in bold), rather than FileReader or FtpReader. It has a constructor that takes in an IReader interface:

```
public class DataReaderClient {
  private IReader reader = null;
  private static String fileName
    = "src/main/resources/basics/basics-trades-data.txt";

  public DataReaderClient(IReader reader) {
    this.reader = reader;
  }

  private String fetchData() {
    return reader.read();
  }

  public static void main(String[] args) {
    ...
  }
}
```

Looking at the client code, if I ask you to tell me the actual reader that has been used by the client, would you be able to tell me? You can't!

The DataReaderClient does not know where it is fed the data until runtime. The IReader class will only be resolved at runtime by using polymorphism. All we know is that the client can get any of the concrete implementations of IReader interface. The interface methods that were implemented in concrete incarnations of IReader are invoked appropriately.

The challenge is to provide the appropriate concrete implementations of IReader to the client. One way to do this is to create an instance of IReader in the client program—a FileReader is created and passed on to the client as shown here:

```
public class DataReaderClient {
  private IReader reader = null;
  private static String fileName
    = "src/main/resources/basics/basics-trades-data.txt";
    ...
  public static void main(String[] args) {
    IReader fileReader = new FileReader(fileName);// Ummh..still hard wired?
    DataReaderClient client = new DataReaderClient(fileReader);
    System.out.println("Got data using interface design priciple: "
        + client.fetchData());
  }
}
```

Well, it is still hardwired as the client should have to know about which IReader it is going to use. Of course, we could swap FileReader with DatabaseReader or FtpRead er without much hassle, as they all implement `IReader` interface. So, we are in a much better position when our Manager comes along and changes his mind!

However, we still have the concrete `IReader` coupled to the client. Ideally, we should eliminate this coupling as much as possible. The question is how can we provide an instance of `IReader` to `DataReaderClient` without hardwiring? Is there a way we can abstract the creation of this `FileReader` away from the client?

Before I ask you more questions, let me tell you the answer: yes! Any *Dependency Injection (DI)* framework can do this job for us. One such framework is Spring Framework.

The Spring Framework is one of the Dependency Injection (or Inversion of Control) frameworks that provides the dependencies to your objects at runtime very elegantly. I won't explain the framework details yet, because we are eager to find the solution to the IReader problem using Spring Framework first.

Introducing Spring

The object interaction is a part and parcel of software programs. The good design allows you to replace the moving parts with no or minimal impact to the existing code. We say the objects are coupled tightly when the moving parts are knitted closely together. However, this type of design is inflexible—it is in a state where it cannot be scalable or testable in isolation or even maintainable without some degree of code change.

Spring Framework can come to the rescue in designing the components and eliminating dependencies.

Dependency Injection

Spring Framework works on one single mantra: *Dependency Injection*. This is sometimes interchangeable with the *Inversion of Control* (IoC) principle.

When a standalone program starts, it starts the main program, creates the dependencies, and then proceeds to execute the appropriate methods. However, this is exactly the reverse if IoC is applied. That is, all the dependencies and relationships are created by the IoC container and then they are injected into the main program as properties. The program is then ready for action. This is essentially the reverse of usual program creation, thus the name *Inversion of Control* principle.

Refactoring IReader by Using the Framework

Coming back to our `IReader` program, the solution is to *inject* a concrete implementation of `IReader` into the client on demand.

Let's modify the client program—see the decoupled client code here:

```java
public class DecoupledDataReaderClient {
  private IReader reader = null;
  private ApplicationContext ctx = null;

  public DecoupledDataReaderClient() {
    ctx = new ClassPathXmlApplicationContext("basics-reader-beans.xml");
  }

  private String fetchData() {
    reader = (IReader) ctx.getBean("reader");
    return reader.read();
  }

  public static void main(String[] args) {
    DecoupledDataReaderClient client = new DecoupledDataReaderClient();
    System.out.println("Example 1.3: Got data: " + client.fetchData());
  }
}
```

As we can see, there is lots of magic going on in this class—the magician being the ApplicationContext class! Let's see briefly what's going on in there.

When the class is instantiated by the JVM, Spring Framework's `ClassPathXmlApplica tionContext` object is created in the class's constructor. This context class reads a configuration XML file and creates any objects declared in that file—a `FileReader` by the name of "reader" bean in this case. The instantiation of the `ApplicationContext` creates the *container* that consists of the objects defined in that XML file. When the fetchData is invoked, the same reader bean is fetched from the container and the appropriate methods on the `FileReader` were executed.

Don't worry if you didn't get much of it, you will learn about them in no time, trust me! We will discuss the framework fundamentals later in the chapter, but for now, let's continue with our reader example.

After creating the client class, create a XML file that consists of definitions of our `FileReader`. The XML file is shown here:

```xml
<?xml version="1.0" encoding="UTF-8"?>
<beans xmlns="http://www.springframework.org/schema/beans"
       xmlns:xsi="http://www.w3.org/2001/XMLSchema-instance"
       xsi:schemaLocation="http://www.springframework.org/schema/beans
        http://www.springframework.org/schema/beans/spring-beans.xsd">

    <bean name="reader" class="com.madhusudhan.jscore.basics.FileReader">
        <constructor-arg value
            ="src/main/resources/basics/basics-trades-data.txt" />
    </bean>

</beans>
```

The purpose of this XML file is to create the respective beans (instances of our classes) and their relationships. This XML file is then provided to the `ApplicationContext` instance, which creates a container with these beans and their object graphs along with relationships.

Looking at the reader bean in the preceding configuration file, the `ctx = new ClasspathXmlApplicationContext("basics-reader-beans.xml")` statement creates a container to hold the beans defined in the *basics-reader-beans.xml*. The `FileReader` class is created by the framework with a name `reader` and stored in this container. The Spring container is simply a holder for the bean instances that were created from the XML file. An API is provided to query these beans and use them accordingly from our client application.

For example, using the API method `ctx.getBean("reader")`, you can access the respective bean instances. That's exactly what we are doing in our client, in the `fetchData` method by using the statement: `reader = (IReader) ctx.getBean("reader");`

The bean obtained is a fully instantiated `FileReader` bean, so you can invoke the methods normally: `reader.read()`.

So, to wrap up, here are the things that we have done to make our program work without dependencies by using Spring:

- We have implemented `IReader` creating a `FileReader` class as a simple POJO.
- We have created a simple XML configuration file to declare this bean.
- We then created a container (using the ApplicationContext) with this single bean by reading the XML file.
- We queried the container to obtain our fully qualified instance of the FileReader class so we can invoke the respective methods.

Simple and straightforward, eh?

One quick note to the curious here: usually we use the `new` operator to create a brand new Object in Java. In the above client code, you don't see us using `new` operator to create a FileReader. The framework has taken over this responsibility for us—it creates these objects by peeking at the declared definitions in the XML configuration file.

Before we wind up the chapter, there's one more thing we should look at. The client and the reader are still coupled! That is, the client will always be injected with a type of `IReader` defined in configuration. Ideally, the client should not have to know about the `IReader`—instead, we can have a service layer to disassociate the reader with the client. This way the service would be glued to the client rather than the `IReader`. Let's do this by creating a service.

ReaderService

The `ReaderService` is a simple class which abstracts away the implementation details of the `IReader` from the client. The client will only have knowledge of the service; it will know nothing about where the service is going to get the data from. The first step is to write the service. This snippet is the our new service class:

```
public class ReaderService {
  private IReader reader = null;

  public ReaderService(IReader reader) {
    this.reader = reader;
  }

  public String fetchData() {
    return reader.read();
  }
}
```

The service has a class variable of `IReader` type. It is injected with an `IReader` implementation via the constructor. It has just one method—`fetchData` which delegates the call to a respective implementation to return the data.

The following XML file wires the `ReaderService` with an appropriate `IReader` in our *basics-reader-beans.xml* file:

```
<beans>
  <bean name="readerService"
    class="com.madhusudhan.jscore.basics.service.ReaderService">
    <constructor-arg ref="reader" />
  </bean>

  <bean name="reader"
    class="com.madhusudhan.jscore.basics.readers.FileReader">
    <constructor-arg
      value="src/main/resources/basics/basics-trades-data.txt" />
  </bean>
</beans>
```

When this config file is read by the Spring's `ApplicationContext` in your program, the `ReaderService` and `FileReader` beans are instantiated. Note that, as the `ReaderSer vice` has a reference to a reader (`constructor-arg ref="reader"`), the `FileReader` is instantiated first and injected into `ReaderService`. If for what ever reason the `FileR eader` was not instantiated, the framework throws an exception and quits the program immediately—hence the framework is said to be designed as *fail-fast*.

Here is the modified `ReaderServiceClient`:

```
public class ReaderServiceClient {
  private ApplicationContext ctx = null;
  private ReaderService service =  null;
```

```
  public ReaderServiceClient() {
    ctx = new ClassPathXmlApplicationContext("basics-reader-beans.xml");
    service = (ReaderService) ctx.getBean("readerService");
  }

  private String fetchData() {
    return service.fetchData();
  }

  public static void main(String[] args) {
    ReaderServiceClient client = new ReaderServiceClient();
    System.out.println("Got data using ReaderService: " + client.fetchData());
  }
}
```

The notable thing is that the client will only have knowledge of the service—no Read
ers whatsoever—thus achieving the true decoupling of the software components.

If you wish to read data from a database, remember that except for config, no other code
changes are required—enable an appropriate reader in the config and re-run the program. For example, in the next snippet, the FileReader is now swapped with a Databa
seReader—without changing even single line of code—by just modifying the meta data.

This is shown here:

```
<bean name="readerService"
    class="com.madhusudhan.jscore.basics.service..ReaderService">
  <!-- The reader now refers to DBReader -->
  <property name="reader" ref="reader"/>
</bean>

<!-- *** DBReader ** -->
<bean name="reader"
    class="com.madhusudhan.jscore.basics.readers.DatabaseReader">
    <property name="dataSource" ref="dataSource" />
</bean>

<!-- Datasource that DBReader depends -->
<bean id="dataSource" class="org.apache.commons.dbcp.BasicDataSource">
  ....
</bean>
```

The ReaderService is given a reference to the respective IReader dynamically when
the program is run.

Summary

This chapter introduced the Spring Framework from the 10,000-foot view. We have seen
the problem of object coupling and how the framework solved the dependency issues.

We also glanced at a framework's containers and scratched the surface of the framework's usage, leaving many of the fundamentals to the upcoming chapters.

We are going to see the internals of the framework in depth in the next chapter.

CHAPTER 2

Fundamentals

We saw the bare-minimum basics of Spring Framework in the last chapter. We worked with new things such as beans, bean factories, and containers. This chapter explains them in detail. It discusses writing beans, naming conventions, how they are wired into containers, and so on.

Configuring Beans

For Spring, all objects are beans! The fundamental step in the Spring Framework is to define your objects as beans. Beans are nothing but object instances that would be created and manage by the Spring Framework by looking at their class definitions. These definitions basically form the configuration metadata. The framework then creates a plan for which objects need to be instantiated, which dependencies need to be set and injected, and the scope of the newly created instance, etc., is based on this configuration metadata.

The metadata can be supplied in a simple XML file, as we saw in Chapter 1. Alternatively, one could provide the metadata as annotation or Java Configuration.

We first discover the definitions of the Spring beans by using a config file which is discussed in the next section.

Using XML

We saw earlier that the Framework reads the Java classes defined in the XML config and initializes and loads them as Spring beans into a runtime container. The container is a runtime bucket of all the fully prepared instances of Java classes. Let's take a look at an example of how this process is executed.

We will define a bean with a name `person` that corresponds to a class `Person`. The `Person` has three properties, two of which (`firstName` and `lastName`) were set via the constructor, while the third one (age) is set by using a setter. There is also another property called address. However, this property is not an simple Java type, but instead points (references) to another class Address.

The following snippet shows the Person bean class's definition:

```
public class Person {
  private int age = 0;
  private String firstName = null;
  private String lastName = null;
  private Address address = null;

  public Person(String fName, String lName){
    firstName = fName;
    lastName = lName;
  }
  public int getAge() {
    return age;
  }

  public void setAge(int age) {
    this.age = age;
  }
  public Address getAddress() {
    return address;
  }
  public void setAddress(Address address) {
    this.address = address;
  }
  public String getDetails(){
    return firstName +" "+lastName
      +" is "+getAge()+" old and lives at "+getAddress();
  }
}
```

As you can see, only age and address variables have setters—meaning they are set in a different way than the variables set via constructor. For completeness, the Address class definition is:

```
public class Address {
  private int doorNumber = 0;
  private String firstLine = null;
  private String secondLine = null;
  private String zipCode = null;
  // getters and setters for these variables go here
  ....
}
```

The ultimate goal is to create the Person and Address beans via our configuration files. The classes are declared in a Spring configuration XML file as shown here:

```
<?xml version="1.0" encoding="UTF-8"?>
<beans xmlns="http://www.springframework.org/schema/beans"
```

```xml
        xmlns:xsi="http://www.w3.org/2001/XMLSchema-instance"
        xsi:schemaLocation="http://www.springframework.org/schema/beans
        http://www.springframework.org/schema/beans/spring-beans.xsd">

  <bean name="person" class="com.madhusudhan.jscore.beans.Person">
    <constructor-arg value="Madhusudhan" />
    <constructor-arg value="Konda" />
    <property name="age" value="99"/>
    <property name="address" ref="address"/>
  </bean>

  <bean name="address" class="com.madhusudhan.jscore.beans.Address">
    <property name="doorNumber" value="99"/>
    <property name="firstLine" value="Rainbow Vistas"/>
    <property name="secondLine" value="Kukatpally, Hyderabad"/>
    <property name="zipCode" value="101010"/>
  </bean>
</beans>
```

There are few things that we should take a note of here.

The topmost node declares <beans> as your root element. All bean definitions would then follow using a <bean> tag. Usually, the XML file consists of at least one bean. Each bean definition may contain sets of information, most importantly the name and the class tags. It may also have other information, such as the id, the scope of the bean, the dependencies, and others.

Basically, when the config file is loaded at runtime, the framework will pick up these definitions and create the instance of Person. It then gives a name as person. This name is then used to query for the same instance from the container by using a Framework's API.

For example, the following code snippet illustrates how a PersonClient loads up its container and queries the beans:

```java
public class PersonClient {
  private static ApplicationContext context = null;
  public PersonClient() {
    context = new ClassPathXmlApplicationContext("ch2-spring-beans.xml");
  }
  public String getPersonDetails() {
    Person person =
     (Person) context.getBean("person");
     return person.getDetails();
  }
}
```

From the above snippet, two steps are significant.

- The ApplicationContext is instantiated by an appropriate beans config file. This context is nothing but our bucket of beans—a container in Spring's terminology.

- Querying the container for our newly created Person bean. We use the framework's Context API to search the Java instance, using the getBean() method. The string value that you pass to this getBean() query API method is the name that you've given the bean in your XML file—person in this case.

You can split the bean definitions across multiple files.

For example, you create all the beans that deliver the business functions in a file called *business-beans.xml*, the utility beans in *util-beans.xml*, data access beans in *dao-beans.xml*, and so on. We will see how to instantiate the Spring container by using multiple files later in the chapter.

Generally, I follow the convention of creating the files by using two parts separated by a hyphen. The first part usually represents the business function, while the second part simply indicates that these are spring beans. There is no restriction on the naming convention, so feel free to name your beans whatever you like.

Each bean should either have a name or id field attached to it. You can create the beans with neither of these things, making them anonymous beans (which are not available to query in your client code). The name and id fields both serve the same purpose, except that the id field corresponds to XML specification's id notation. This means that checks are imposed on the id (for example, no special characters in the id value). The name field does not attract any of these restrictions.

The class field declares the fully qualified name of the class. If the instantiation of the class requires any initialization data, it is set via properties or a constructor argument.

For example, in the above XML file, the Person object is instantiated with both: a constructor argument and property setters. The firstName and lastName were set using the <constructor-arg value="..."/> tag, while the rest of the properties were set using a simple property tag: <property name="age" value=".."/>.

The value fields can be simple values or references to other beans. A ref tag is used if a the bean needs another bean, as is seen for address: <property name="address" ref="address"/> . Note the use of ref keyword rather than value keyword when another bean is referenced.

You can name the bean as you wish. However, I would suggest sticking to a camelCase class name, with the first letter lowercase.

Using Annotations

One possible way of Spring wiring is using annotations. When you choose to go along the path of annotations to define your beans and wire them, you are effectively reducing your XML meta data configurations.

Let's see how we can define beans using annotations. The ReservationManager has one dependency—a ReservationService. The sevice property must be injected into our manager to do its flight reservation work.

The dummy service definition is shown here:

```
public class ReservationService {
    public void doReserve(ReservationMessage msg){
        //
    }
}
```

The ResevationManager has a dependency—it needs the reservation service so it process the flight reservations. In order to fulfil this dependency, we need to inject the service into the manager. Unlike the config route, we will inject this dependency by using an annotation called @Autowired annotation. See how we decorated the variable reservationService, using this annotation shown in the following snippet:

```
public class ReservationManager {
    @Autowired
    private ReservationService reservationService = null;

    public void process(Reservation r) {
        reservationService.reserve(r);
    }
}
```

When a variable, method or constructor is annotated with @Autowired, framework will find the relevant dependency and inject that dependency automatically. In the preceding case, the ReservationManager is looking for a ReservationService instance. Behind the scenes, the framework will wire the bean by finding it byType (check the autowiring section for more details).

One last thing we need to do is let framework know we are going to use annotations. The way we do this is to declare a special tag in the XML file:

```
<beans xmlns="http://www.springframework.org/schema/beans"
       xmlns:xsi="http://www.w3.org/2001/XMLSchema-instance"
       xmlns:context="http://www.springframework.org/schema/context"
       xsi:schemaLocation="http://www.springframework.org/schema/beans
       http://www.springframework.org/schema/beans/spring-beans.xsd
       http://www.springframework.org/schema/context
       http://www.springframework.org/schema/context/spring-context.xsd">

    <context:annotation-config/>
    <!-- our reservation service -->
    <bean name="resSvcABC"
        class="com.madhusudhan.jscore.fundamentals.annotations.ReservationService"/>
    <bean name="reservationManager"
        class="com.madhusudhan.jscore.fundamentals.annotations.ReservationManager"/>
</beans>
```

The annotation-config tag lets the framework know we are following the annotations route. This way, it starts searching for the classes that may have the appropriate annotations (in our case, we have ReservationManager with @Autowired annotation) and do fulfil any obligations.

Note that we need to import appropriate context schemas as shown in bold in the above snippet.

When ReservationManger gets created, the framework looks for a ReservationService type bean (we have created one in the bean config) and injects it. I have deliberately set the name of the service bean to resSvsABC so you would know that framework uses byType rather than byName when picking up the dependencies.

When the reservationManager gets created, it will always be injected with the service bean!

There are couple of things that we should look at.

We did not declare any properties on the ReservationManager, for example, <property name="reservationService" ref="resSvs"/>, as we would do normally. There are no setters and getters on the ReservationManager too. This is all redundant because the job is cleanly done by the annotation configuration!

Before we close this section, there's another attribute that we should see—the component-scan attribute on the context namespace.

In the previous snippet, although we have eliminated much of XML, we still had to define the service bean in the XML. Is there a way we could avoid this and condense our XML further?

Yes, we should use the component-scan attribute that gobbles away much of our XML. As the tag may indicate, component-scan basicaly scans a particular drectory or directories to find out special annotated classes.

Revisiting the ReservationService, annotate the class by using the @Component annotation:

```
@Component
public class ReservationService {
  ..
}
```

Any class annotated with this @Component annotation will be picked up by the framework (as long as the class is the part of the component-scan's base-package value) and gets instantiated. The next thing we need to do is to declare the component-scan as shown here:

```
<context:component-scan
  base-package="com.madhusudhan.jscore.fundamentals.annotations"/>
```

By declaring this tag, what we are telling the framework is to search all the annotated (with @Component) classes in the package indicated by base-package attribute. Hence ReservationService will be searched for and instantiated by the framework and gets injected into the ReservationManager bean because of @Autowired annotation.

If you do not wish to tie up to Spring's @Autowired annotation usage, perhaps think about using JSR-330's @Inject annotation. Spring supports this annotation too. Although we can't discuss @Inject annotation here, it is almost replica of @Autowired annotation.

There's a lot of debate on using annotations against XML configurations. Although annotations do not clutter our XML files, they are tied to the source. There are various schools of thought, some encouraging while others are discouraging the use of annotations. Personally, I like annotations and their clean and neat approach to solving configuration issues. However, I prefer to use meta-data for the simple reason that I can change the configuration without having to recompile/rebuild the application.

XML Namespaces

Sometimes the configuration files seems to have lot of bean information. This is an eyesore to readers at times. However, the good news is that they can be condensed by using schema-based XML configuration. We have been using XML Schemas all along in as the following meta data snippet illustrates:

```
<?xml version="1.0" encoding="UTF-8"?>
<beans xmlns="http://www.springframework.org/schema/beans"
       xmlns:xsi="http://www.w3.org/2001/XMLSchema-instance"
       xsi:schemaLocation="http://www.springframework.org/schema/beans
       http://www.springframework.org/schema/beans/spring-beans-3.0.xsd">
  <!-- declare your beans here -->
  <bean>
              ...
  </bean>
</beans>
```

As you can see, the beans schema has been used in the above configuration. Spring defines various schemas such as jms, aop, jee, tx, lang, util, and others.

Adding the appropriate schemas is quite straightforward. For example, if you are going to use a jms schema, add the following lines (in bold) to the configuration:

```
<?xml version="1.0" encoding="UTF-8"?>
<beans xmlns="http://www.springframework.org/schema/beans"
       xmlns:xsi="http://www.w3.org/2001/XMLSchema-instance"
       xmlns:jms="http://www.springframework.org/schema/jms"
       xmlns:context="http://www.springframework.org/schema/context"
       xsi:schemaLocation="http://www.springframework.org/schema/beans
       http://www.springframework.org/schema/beans/spring-beans-3.0.xsd
```

```
      http://www.springframework.org/schema/jms
      http://www.springframework.org/schema/jms/spring-jms-3.0.xsd">
      ....
</beans>
```

A xmlns tag defines a jms namespace while the last two line indicate the location of the schema definitions. So, replace the xxx shown in the following pattern with a specific schema you wish to import:

```
<!-- Replace xxx with one of the many schemas such as jms, aop, tx etc -->
http://www.springframework.org/schema/xxx
http://www.springframework.org/schema/xxx/spring-xxx-3.0.xsd
```

Once you have the appropriate schema and the associated namespace (using the xmlns tag), using the schema-based configuration is a breeze.

```
<?xml version="1.0" encoding="UTF-8"?>
<beans xmlns="http://www.springframework.org/schema/beans"
       xmlns:xsi="http://www.w3.org/2001/XMLSchema-instance"
       xmlns:jms="http://www.springframework.org/schema/jms"
       xsi:schemaLocation="http://www.springframework.org/schema/beans
       http://www.springframework.org/schema/beans/spring-beans-3.0.xsd
       http://www.springframework.org/schema/jms
       http://www.springframework.org/schema/jms/spring-jms-3.0.xsd">

       <jms:listener-container>
         ...
       </jms:listener-contaner>
</beans>
```

See how the listener-container bean is added to the container by using the jms namespace.

The good old DTD-style configuration is still valid too:

```
<?xml version="1.0" encoding="UTF-8"?>
<!DOCTYPE beans PUBLIC "-//SPRING//DTD BEAN//EN"
          "http://www.springframework.org/dtd/spring-beans.dtd">
<beans>
  ....
</beans>
```

However, I strongly recommend using the schema-based configuration unless you have a valid reason to stick to older DTD style.

Creating Beans

The beans are instances wired together to achieve an application's goal.

Usually in a standard Java application, we follow a specific life cycle of the components, including their dependencies and associations.

For example, when you start a main class, it automatically creates all the dependencies, sets the properties, and instantiates the dependent instances for your application to progress.

The responsibility of creating the dependency and associating this dependency to the appropriate instance is given to your main class in our standalone application.

However, in Spring, this responsibility is taken away from us and given to the Spring Framework. The instances (a.k.a. beans) are created, the associations are established, and dependencies are injected by the Spring Framework entirely. You and I have no say except in defining and loading them.

So, creating the whole object graph is the responsibility of the framework!

These beans that exists in a container are then queried by the application and act upon them. Of course, you would have to declare these associations and other configuration metadata either in an XML file or provide them as annotations for the Framework to understand what it should do.

One important characteristic of the Framework while creating beans is to follow a *fail-fast* approach.

When the Framework encounters any issues in loading a bean, it just quits—no container with half-baked beans ever gets created. This is a really good characteristic of a framework as it would be forced to catch all errors during compile time rathen than at runtime.

Life Cycle

The Spring Framework does quite a few things behind the scenes.

The life cycle of a bean is easy to understand, yet different from the life cycle exposed in a standard Java application. In a normal Java process, a bean is usually instantiated using a *new* operator. The Framework executes more actions in addition to simply creating the beans. Once they are created, they are loaded into the appropriate container (we will learn about containers in Chapter 3) for a client to access them.

The usual life-cycle steps are listed here:

- The framework factory loads a bean definitions and creates it.
- The bean is then populated with the properties as declared in the bean definitions. If the property is a reference to another bean, the other bean will be created and populated, and the reference is injected into this bean.

- If our bean implements any of the Spring's interfaces, such as `BeanNameAware` or `BeanFactoryAware`, appropriate callback methods will be invoked.
- The framework also invokes any `BeanPostProcessor`'s associated with your bean for pre-initialzation.
- The `init-method`, if specified, is invoked on the bean.
- The post-initialization will be performed if specified on the bean.

Do not get stressed if the things mentioned here don't get digested yet—we will discuss these points in the coming sections in detail.

When comes to creating the beans, beans which have no dependencies will be created normally. Whereas, the beans which has dependencies (that is, some of its properties refer to other beans) will be created only after satisfying the dependencies they have.

We will discuss this process in the next section, using some examples.

Note that we can also create beans by using static methods or Factories. We will look at them in the next chapter in detail.

Instantiating Beans Without Dependencies

Do you remember the `FileReader` class we defined in our earlier chapter? Here's the snippet of the class if you can't recall:

```
public class FileReader implements IReader{
  private StringBuilder builder = null;
  private Scanner scanner = null;

  // constructor
  public FileReader(String fileName) { ... }

  // read method implementation
  public String read() { ... }
}
```

The `FileReader`'s constructor takes in a `fileName` as its argument in order to get ready for the action. This bean is defined by passing an argument to the constructor, using meta-data. Look at the meta data of the bean:

```
<bean name="reader" class="com.madhusudhan.jscore.basics.readers.FileReader">
  <constructor-arg value="src/main/resources/basics/basics-trades-data.txt" />
</bean>
```

The required `fileName` variable is set with a value via the `constructor-arg` tag, providing a value of `src/main/resources/basics/basics-trades-data.txt` as an argument.

When the Framework reads the definition of this class, it creates an instance by using the *new* operator (in reality, the bean is instantiated by using Java Reflection). As this bean has no dependencies, it will now be instantiated and ready to use.

Instantiating Beans With Dependencies

There is a second case where beans depend on other beans. For example, we have seen a `Person` having an `Address`. Unless the `Address` object is created, creating the Person can't be succesful. So, the Person bean is *dependent* on the Address bean. However, if the `FileReader` bean has a dependency on another bean, the other bean will be created and instantiated. See the following snippet.

See the definition of `Person` having an `address` property which refers to another bean named `address`? The Person object will be injected with an Address object to satisfy the dependency. The bean dependencies can be one or more beans.

```
<bean name="person"
  class="com.madhusudhan.jscore.beans.Person">
  ....
  <property name="address" ref="address"/>
</bean>

<bean name="address"
  class="com.madhusudhan.jscore.beans.Address">
  ....
</bean>
```

The order of creation is important to Spring. After digesting the configuration metadata, Spring creates a plan (it allocates certain priorities to each bean) with the order of beans that needs to be created to satisfy dependencies. Hence, the `Address` object is created first, before the `Person`. If Spring encounters any exception while creating the `Ad dress` object, it will fail fast and quit the program. It does not create any further beans and lets the developer know why it won't progress further.

Aliasing Beans

Sometimes, we may need to give the same bean a different name—usually as alias. For example, an Address bean can be called as shipping address or a billing address. Aliasing is a way of naming the same bean with different names. We use the `alias` tag to give a name to a predefined bean.

```
<bean name="address"
  class="com.madhusudhan.jscore.fundamentals.Address">
  ...
</bean>
```

```
<alias name="address" alias="billingAddress"/>
<alias name="address" alias="shippingAddress"/>
```

In the above snippet, we have declared an Address bean with address as it's name. Two aliases, billingAddress and shippingAddress were declared, both pointing to the same bean. We can use either of the aliases in our application as if they were original beans.

Anonymous Beans

We can also create beans whose existence is associated to the referencing bean only. These types of beans are called Anonymous or Inner beans. They are *nameless* and hence not available for our programs to query them.

```
<bean name="reader" class="com.madhusudhan.jscore.basics.readers.FileReader">
  <constructor-arg value="src/main/resources/basics/basics-trades-data.txt" />
  <property name="platformLineEnder"
    <bean class="com.madhusudhan.jscore.basics.readers.WindowsLineEnder"/>
  </property>
</bean>
```

The platformLineEnder property refers to a WindowsLineEnder bean. Because the platformLineEnder bean has been defined as a property (no ref tag is defined), it is not available to any other beans in the context except the FileReader bean.

Injection Types

Spring allows us to inject the properties via constructors or setters. While both types are equally valid and simple, it's a matter of personal preference in choosing one over the other.

One advantage to using constructor types over setters is that we do not have to write additional setter code. Having said that, it is not ideal to create constructors with lots of properties as arguments. I detest writing a class with a constructor that has more than a couple of arguments!

Constructor Type Injection

In the previous examples, we have seen how to inject the properties via constructors by using the constructor-arg attribute. Those snippets illustrate the constructor injection method. The basic idea is that the class will have a constructor that takes the arguments, and these arguments are wired via the config file.

Here is an FtpReader code snippet that has a constructor taking two arguments:

```
public class FtpReader implements IReader {
  private String ftpHost = null;
```

```
    private int ftpPort = 0;

    public FtpReader(String ftpHost, int ftpPort) {
      this.ftpHost = ftpHost;
      this.ftpPort = ftpPort;
    }

    @Override
    public String read() {
      // your impl goes here
      return null;
    }
  }
```

The ftpHost and ftpPort arguments are then wired using constructor-arg attributes defined in the XML config file:

```
<bean name="reader" class="com.madhusudhan.jscore.basics.readers.FtpReader">
  <constructor-arg value="madhusudhan.com" />
  <constructor-arg value="10009" />
</bean>
```

You can set references to other beans, too via the constructor arguments. For example, the following snippet injects a reference FileReader into the ReaderService constructor:

```
<bean name="readerService"
    class="com.madhusudhan.jscore.basics.service.ReaderService">
  <constructor-arg ref="reader" />
</bean>

<bean name="reader" class="com.madhusudhan.jscore.basics.readers.FileReader">
  <constructor-arg value="src/main/resources/basics/basics-trades-data.txt" />
</bean>
```

This is how the ReaderService will look with a constructor accepting an IReader type:

```
public class ReaderService {
  private IReader reader = null;

  public ReaderService(IReader reader) {
    this.reader = reader;
  }
  ...
}
```

Argument type resolution

One quick note about constructor type injection—there are couple of rules that framework will follow when resolving the types of the arguments. In the preceding FtpReader example, the first argument was ftpHost followed by ftpPort. The case is straightforward—the constructor expects a string and an integer, so the framework picks the first argument as String type and the second one as Integer type.

Although you declare them as string values in your config file (such as `value=".."`), the `java.beans.PropertyEditor`'s are used by the framework to convert the string value to the appropriate property type.

Ideally, the declaration should define the types too as shown in the following snippet:

```
<bean name="reader" class="com.madhusudhan.jscore.basics.readers.FtpReader">
    <constructor-arg type="String" value="madhusudhan.com" />
    <constructor-arg type="int" value="10009" />
</bean>
```

The types are normal Java types—such as `int`, `boolean`, `double`, `String`, and so on.

You could also set index's on the values, starting the index from zero as shown here:

```
<bean name="reader" class="com.madhusudhan.jscore.basics.readers.FtpReader">
    <constructor-arg index="0" type="String" value="madhusudhan.com" />
    <constructor-arg index="1" type="int" value="10009" />
</bean>
```

Setter Type Injection

In addition to injecting the dependent beans and properties via constructors, Spring also allows them to be injected via setters, too. In order to use the setter injection, we have to provide setters on the respective variables. If the property exhibits read and write characteristics, provide both a setter and a getter on the variable.

So, in our `ReaderService` class, create a variable of `IReader` type and a matching setter/getter for that property. The constructor is left empty as the properties are now populated using the setters. You should follow the normal bean conventions when creating setters and getters.

Modified `ReaderService` is given here:

```
public class ReaderService {
  private IReader reader = null;

  // Setter and getter
  public void setReader(IReader reader) {
    this.reader = reader;
  }

  public IReader getReader() {
    return reader;
  }
  ...
}
```

The significant points are the the setter and getter methods on the IReader variable and the omission of the constructor altogether. The configuration of the class in our XML file looks like this:

```
<bean name="readerService"
    class="com.madhusudhan.jscore.basics.service.ReaderService">
  <!-- Setter type injection -->
  <property name="reader" ref="reader"/>
</bean>

<bean name="reader" class="com.madhusudhan.jscore.basics.readers.FileReader">
  ...
</bean>
```

The notable change is to create a property called reader and set it with a reference to the FileReader class. The framework will check the ReaderService for a reader property and invoke setReader by passing the FileReader instance.

Mixing Constructor and Setter

You can mix and match the injection types as you like, too. The revised FileReader class listed here has a constructor as well as few other properties. The componentName is set using setter, while the fileName is injected via constuctor.

```
<bean name="reader"
    class="com.madhusudhan.jscore.fundamentals.injection.FileReader">
  <constructor-arg value="src/main/resources/basics/basics-trades-data.txt" />
  <property name="componentName" value="TradeFileReader"/>
</bean>
```

Although mixing and matching the injection types is absolutely possible, I recommend sticking with one or the other of them, rather than both, to avoid complicating matters.

Bean Callbacks

Spring Framework provides a couple of hooks to our beans in the form of callback methods. These methods provide opportunity for the bean to initialize properties or clean up resources. There are two such method hooks: init-method and destroy-method.

init-method

When a bean is being created, we can let Spring invoke a specific method on our bean to initialize. This method provides a chance for the bean to do housekeeping stuff and any initialization, such as creating data structures, creating thread pools, and so on.

Say we have a requirement of creating a class for fetching Foreign Exchange (FX) rates. The FxRateProvider is a class that provides us with these rates when queried (mind you, it's a dummy implementation of FX Rates!).

See the code snippet here:

```
public class FxRateProvider {
  private double rate = 0.0;
  private String baseCurrency = "USD";
  private Map<String, Double> currencies = null;

  /* Invoked via Spring's init-method callback */
  public void initMe(){
    currencies = new HashMap<String, Double>();
    currencies.put("GBP",1.5);
    currencies.put("USD",1.0);
    currencies.put("JPY", 1000.0);
    currencies.put("EUR",1.4);
    currencies.put("INR",50.00);
  }

  public double getRate(String currency){
   if(!currencies.containsKey(currency))
     return 0;
   return currencies.get(currency);
  }
}
```

A noticeable point is the initMe method. It is a normal method invoked by the Framework during the process of its creation.

The associated configuration of the bean is provided in the following XML:

```
<bean name="fxRateProvider"
  class="com.madhusudhan.jscore.fundamentals.callbacks.FxRateProvider"
  init-method="initMe">
  <property name="baseCurrency" value="USD"/>
</bean>
```

destroy-method

Similar to the initialization, framework provides a destroy method to clean up before destroying the bean—named as destroy-method. The FxRateProvider shown here has a destroy method:

```
public class FxRateProvider {

  public void destroyMe() {
    // do your cleanup operations here
    currencies = null;
  }
```

```
...
}
```

We should refer the `destroyMe` method in the XML declaration like this:

```
<bean name="fxRateProvider"
    class="com.madhusudhan.jscore.fundamentals.callbacks.FxRateProvider"
    init-method="initMe"
    destroy-method="destroyMe">

    <property name="baseCurrency" value="USD"/>
</bean>
```

When the program quits, the framework destroys the beans. During the process of destruction, when the config metadata declares `destroyMe` as the destroy method, the `destroyMe` method is invoked. This gives the bean a chance to do some housekeeping activities if we wish.

Ideally, this method should be coded to free up resources, nullify objects, and other cleanup operations.

Common Callbacks

Let's say we religiously code a `init` and `destroy` methods on all our beans. Does it mean we have to declare the `init-method` and `destroy-method` explicitly on each and every bean? Well, not exactly.

As long as we define the same method names across all the beans, we can use Framework's facility of declaring default callbacks—`default-init-method` and `default-destroy-method`.

Instead of declaring the individual methods on each of the bean, we need to declare these default callbacks at the topmost `beans` element. See how they have been declared in the following XML snippet:

```
<beans xmlns="http://www.springframework.org/schema/beans"
       xmlns:xsi="http://www.w3.org/2001/XMLSchema-instance"
       xsi:schemaLocation="http://www.springframework.org/schema/beans
       http://www.springframework.org/schema/beans/spring-beans.xsd"
       default-init-method="initMe"
       default-destroy-method="destroyMe" >
   <bean>
   ...
   </bean>
</beans>
```

Note that these default methods are associated to the `beans` element rather than a bean element.

From the above example, the `initMe` and `destroyMe` methods will be invoked automaticaly on all the beans. If any of the beans don't have these methods, Framework ignores them and no action is performed.

Summary

This chapter discussed the Spring Framework in detail. It explained the concept of beans and bean factories. We have also learned about the life cycle of the bean scopes and touched upon the property editors used in injecting Java Collections and other types of objects.

We discuss the containers and application contexts in the next chapter, which forms a crucial concept in putting the framework to work.

CHAPTER 3

Containers

A Spring container is the backbone of the framework. A container is basically a pool of beans created in a memory space by the framework when the application starts up. An API provided by the framework exposes methods to query these beans from the container.

We'll start the chapter by looking at the containers and different categories. We'll also look at details about concepts such as AutoWiring.

Containers

Understanding containers is an important task when working with the Spring Framework as they are crucial moving pieces in a Spring's jig-saw puzzle.

During the startup process, the beans are instantiated, the associations and relationships are created, all the relationships are satisfied, and dependencies are injected. All named beans are available for querying using an API. Some beans are lazily loaded while others are loaded during the initialization of the container. This means that unless the bean is requested by our application or some other bean (as a part of dependency), the framework will not instantiate the bean, except loading singletons.

Spring containers primarily fall into two categories: *Bean Factories* and *Application Contexts*—supported by the `BeanFactory` and `ApplicationContext` classes respectively. The names are sort of misnomers, as they do not give any clue as to what these containers are and what they do.

The `BeanFactory` is a simple container supporting basic dependency injection, whereas `ApplicationContext` is an extension of `BeanFactory`, which has few additional bells and whistles.

In my personal opinion, I would vote for using `ApplicationContext` over `BeanFactory` —I'll tell you why in the next few sections!

BeanFactory Container

The `BeanFactory` is the simplest of the two types of containers Spring has provided. The concrete factories must implement the `org.springframework.beans.facto ry.BeanFactory` interface. This factory creates and instantiates beans with all the dependent configurations as expected. So, when you query a bean, it is obtained in your client as a fully functional instance, meaning all the associations and relationships have already been created. The bean factory implementor can also invoke the customized `init-method` and the `destroy-method`.

Spring provides a few of the implementations of `BeanFactory` out of the box, the most common being `XmlBeanFactory`. As the name suggests, it reads the configuration metadata from a XML file, basically information about our beans.

Using the `XmlBeanFactory` in a client is very easy and straightforward. The following snippet shows the code demonstrating how to instantiate the factory. The constructor takes in an XML file passed into a `FileInputStream` object:

```
// Instantiate the factory with your beans config file
BeanFactory factory = XmlBeanFactory(new FileInputStream("trade-beans.xml"));

// Use the factory to obtain your TradeService bean
TradeService service = (TradeService) factory.getBean("tradeService");
```

The `BeanFactory` is usually preferred in small device applications such as mobile phones, etc, where resources are limited. If you are writing any standard Java or JEE application, ideally you would ditch `BeanFactory` to go with `ApplicationContext` implementation. I recommend using the `ApplicationContext` container unless you have a strong reason not to.

ApplicationContext Container

The `ApplicationContext` extends the `BeanFactory`, thus all the functionality of `Bean Factory` is already embedded in the `ApplicationContext` container. It also provides some advanced features such as application events, aspect functionality, and a few others as an added bonus. Ideally, we can use this container straight away due to its extended functionality.

Similar to `BeanFactory` implementations, there are few implementations of `Applica tionContext` that will soon be our favorites:

- `FileSystemXmlApplicationContext`: This container loads the definitions of the beans found in the XML file located in a specified file system location. You should provide the path of the beans file to the constructor. This container will most likely be used if we have an application that has a specific location to load the config files rather than bundling them along with the deployed code.

- ClassPathXmlApplicationContext: In this container, the XML config file is read from the classpath by the container. As long as the config file is anywhere in the classpath of our application, this container can load it. You can also have the bean files in a jar file.

  The only difference between the FileSystemXmlApplicationContext and the ClassPathXmlApplicationContext is that this context does not require the full path of the file, but expects to be in the classpath of the application.

- WebXmlApplicationContext: This container loads the bean definitions file within a web application. This context is used mostly in Spring MVC projects or Java Web applications.

We have seen the usage of the ApplicationContext type containers in the earlier chapters, but let's recap the usage again here. The ClassPathXmlApplicationContext is instantiated with a set of bean config files.

For example, the following snippet creates the container by loading the *containers-beans.xml* file.

```
ApplicationContext ctx =
  new ClassPathXmlApplicationContext("containers-beans.xml");
Employee employee =
  ctx.getBean("employee",Employee.class);
```

The snippet also shows the mechanism of querying the Employee bean.

If we have to create our container with multiple config files, we instantiate the constructor with an array of Strings:

```
public class ApplicationContextClient {
  private String[] configLocations =
    new String[]{"containers-beans.xml","fundamentals-beans.xml"};

  public void testClasspathXmlApplicationContext(){
    ctx = new ClassPathXmlApplicationContext(configLocations);

    Employee employee = ctx.getBean("employee",Employee.class);
    Person person = ctx.getBean("person", Person.class);
    System.out.println(employee);
    System.out.println(person);
  }
  ...
}
```

Please check the API documentation for various other ways of creating the container.

The FileSystemXmlApplicationContext is no different from the ClassPathXmlApplicationContext—it accepts a config file with a file path. The following code snippet shows the mechanism to create the FileSystemXmlApplicationContext container:

```
ApplicationContext ctx =
new FileSystemXmlApplicationContext("/src/main/resources/containers-beans.xml");

Employee employee = ctx.getBean("employee",Employee.class);
```

The choice of picking one container over the other depends on your application deployment and environment setup across the organization. Some organizations tend to support a central location for all the config files—this way, the config can be changed or tweaked without having to rebuild and re-deploy the application. Because the file location is static, the FileSystemXmlApplicationContext is best suited in this case.

Some projects may not have to read the configuration data from a centralized location, but the config files are bundled and jarred up with the project itself. The ClassPathXmlApplicationContext is the preferred choice in this case. As you may have already noticed, I have used ClassPathXmlApplicationContext extensively in this book.

Instantiating Beans

Beans are instantiated by the framework in more than one way. We have already seen in previous chapters how the beans were instantiated using constructors. You should ideally provide a constructor in your bean and corresponding metadata in the XML file. If the constructor takes any arguments, we should pass them as constructor-arg attributes in our config file. We will look into two other types of instantiating the beans —using static methods and factories.

Using Static Methods

There may be instances where we need to use static methods on some classes to create their instances—the one pattern that comes to mind immediately is a Java Singleton. The framework provides this mechanism of creating the instances via the exposed static methods rather than constructors. This type of instantiating is well suited if your classes have static factories for creating the object instances.

The procedure is simple: we write a class with a static method that would create an instance of that class. The following snippet shows an EmployeeFactory class. This class follows the Java singleton pattern—a private constructor and a static method instantiator.

```
public class EmployeeFactory {
  private static EmployeeFactory instance;
  private EmployeeFactory() { }
  public static EmployeeFactory getEmployeeFactory() {
    if (instance == null) {
      instance = new EmployeeFactory();
    }
    return instance;
  }
```

```
  ...
}
```

The static `getEmployeeFactory()` returns the instance of this class.

Now that our class with a static method is ready, the next step is to define the bean in our config. The configuration of the bean is similar to the ones we did earlier except that we add an additional attribute `factory-method` on the bean .

Let's see how we can declare a `EmployeeFactory` in the XML file, using the `factory-method` attribute:

```
<bean name="employeeFactory"
  class="com.madhusudhan.jscore.containers.factory.EmployeeFactory"
  factory-method="getEmployeeFactory">
</bean>
```

The `factory-method` attribute invokes the respective static method on the class—the `EmployeeFactory` instance will be instantiated by calling the `factory-method`'s `getEmployeeFactory` method.

Note that the declaration does not mention the `factory-method` being static anywhere. However, it must be declared static if you wish to encounter no errors. Also note that the return type method is not imperative (it should return a non-void value); it is only known if you see the implementation of that method in the declared class, unfortunately.

Using Factory Methods

In the previous section, we created an object, using a static method. What if we wish to create the instance by using non-static methods?

Spring Framework does allow us to instantiate the beans by using non-static factory methods, too. Although it's not straightforward, it's not hard either to grasp.

The `EmployeeCreator` is a simple class that creates either employees or executives by using two factory methods. See the following code snippet:

```
public class EmployeeCreator {
  public Employee createEmployee() {
    return new Employee();
  }
  public Employee createExecutive() {
    Employee emp = new Employee();
    emp.setTitle("EXEC");
    emp.setGrade("GRADE-A");
    return emp;
  }
}
```

The main crux of using factory methods is in the configuration. The `EmployeeCreator` bean is declared as a normal bean. The two other beans—employee and executive are declared using two attributes—factory-bean and factory-method. See the snippet here before we understand the details:

```
<bean name="employee"
    factory-bean="employeeCreator" factory-method="createEmployee"/>
<bean name="executive"
    factory-bean="employeeCreator" factory-method="createExecutive"/>

<!-- the EmployeeCreator bean used by the above two beans -->
<bean name="employeeCreator"
    class="com.madhusudhan.jscore.containers.factory.EmployeeCreator"/>
```

The factory-bean attribute declared on the employee and executive beans both refer to the employeeCreator bean. This is the convention to be followed when working with non-static factory methods. The factory-method points to the actual method on the employeeCreator (factory bean)—in this case, the createEmployee and createExecutive methods on the EmployeeCreator class.

You should have noticed that we do not include the class attribute in the bean definition at all. Take away points are that the actual bean is referred by factory-bean attribute, the respective methods by factory-method attribute. Also, the factory methods are not static in the above implementation.

Initialization and Destruction Callbacks

In our earlier chapter, we have learned that init-method and destroy-method attributes dictate the bean initialization and destruction. These methods will allow us to do some housekeeping jobs during the bean's lifecycle. As you may have noticed, these attributes are used in the configuration but not in our source code.

We may wish to implement such behavior on the beans programatically too. In such cases, the Spring Framework provides us with this functionality by allowing us to implement our classes with two interfaces—the InitializingBean and DisposableBean interfaces. There is one method each in these interfaces—the afterPropertiesSet and destroy methods, respectively.

InitializingBean's afterPropertiesSet

The LazyEmployee wishes to work only THREE days a week—the weekDays variable representing this state is set via configuration on the lazyEmployee bean. See the bean definition here:

```
<bean name="lazyEmployee"
    class="com.madhusudhan.jscore.containers.lifecycle.LazyEmployee">
  <property name="weekDays" value="THREE"/>
</bean>
```

When the bean is intialized, the value is set to THREE as expected. However, someone wishes to override this functionality (perhaps, the LazyEmployee's boss!) resetting it to FIVE days—this reset has to be done after the bean has been created. In this case, the InitializingBean's afterPropertiesSet comes to rescue.

What we need to do is to implement our LazyEmployee class with the Initializing Bean interface—like this:

```
public class LazyEmployee implements InitializingBean {
  private String weekDays = null;

  public void afterPropertiesSet() throws Exception {
    System.out.println("AfterPropertiesSet called");
    weekDays = "FIVE";
  }
  ...
}
```

The interface has only one method, afterPropertiesSet, that needs to be implemented. This method is called *after* all the properties are set and bean is created. Note that the values of these properties are picked up from the config file. In this case, the week Days value was already set in the XML file with THREE. However, before handing over the already created bean to us, the framework called the afterPropertiesSet method which reset the value to FIVE.

In essence, implementing the InitializingBean interface provides the opportunity to initialize (or reset) the bean's configuration.

DisposableBean's destroy

The DisposableBean interface has only one callback method—destroy—which will be called before the Spring container shuts down—thus giving an opportunity to do cleanup of the resources if any.

Continuing with the same example of LazyEmployee, this time, the class implements the DisposableBean interface and its one method, destroy. The souce code is shown in the following snippet:

```
public class LazyEmployee implements DisposableBean {
  private String weekDays = null;

  public void destroy() throws Exception {
    System.out.println("Destroy called");
    // do your cleanup here
  }
  ...
}
```

When the context is closed by calling the `close` method on the `ClassPathXmlApplicationContext` class, the destroy method will be invoked—thus giving us the chance to perform housekeeping before the bean gets reclaimed.

Declarative or Programmatic Callbacks?

We know that there are two options for bean initialization or destruction functionality. We can use `init-method` (or `destroy-method`) by declaring them in configuration files. Or, we can achieve the same result by implementing the `InitialzingBean`'s `afterPropertiesSet` (or `DispozableBean`'s `destroy`) method in our class.

Let me tell you—there's another way of doing this job too—using `@PostConstruct` and `@PreDestroy` annotations. We might see these annotations in action when we learn about annotations in the coming chapters.

You might be wondering what is the preferred option? My vote is always to the configuration side. In the programmatic callbacks, what we are doing is using the Spring's interfaces—thus coupling our code to a third-party dependency. This restricts our future migration plans—should you wish to move to some other Dependency Injection framework (say, Google's Guice), you would have to refactor the code to remove these dependencies.

Remember, the rule of thumb is to avoid vendor lockins as much as possible!

Spring allows us to use all the three types of callbacks that we have discussed so far. But there is a subtle difference if you use all of them in a project—the precedence of one over the other. Spring dictates that if all three types (annotation, programmatic, and config callbacks) are present, the order in which they take precedence is:

1. Annotation based—`@PostConstruct` and `@PreDestroy`
2. Programming based—`afterPropertiesSet` and `destroy`
3. Config based—the `init-method` and `destroy-method`

Event Handling

Sometimes, we may want to react to an event that happened in the container so we can do some custom processing. For example, we want our `FilePoller` component to start polling a directory for incoming files *after* our container was started. Framework has a mechanism to notify us when the context has been started (or stopped). We'll see the mechanics of this in a minute.

There may be a requirement to publish some messages from our beans too—for example, the `FilePoller` might notify interested parties to say that it has received a file or it has processed an encrypted file, and so on. The Spring framework provides a way to publish and listen to the custom events too.

The ApplicationContext publishes certain types of events when loading the beans. For example, a ContextStartedEvent is published when the context is started and Context StoppedEvent is published when the context is stopped. We can have our beans receive these events if we wish to do some processing on our side based on these events. We can also publish our own events.

Let's see the procedure involved in listening to the events first.

Listening to Context Events

The ApplicationContext publishes certain types of events when loading the beans. For example, a ContextStartedEvent is published when the context is started and Context StoppedEvent is published when the context is stopped.

We can let our beans receive these events to do some processing based on these events. In order to listen to the context events, our bean should implement the Application Listener interface. This interface has just one method: onApplicationEvent(Appli cationEvent event). The ContextStartedEventListener is one such class that expects to receive any events related to context's startup actions.

The following example creates this class:

```
public class ContextStartedEventListener
  implements ApplicationListener<ContextStartedEvent> {
  public void onApplicationEvent(ContextStartedEvent event) {
    System.out.println(
    "Received ContextStartedEvent application event:"+event.getSource());
  }
}
```

Whenever the ContextStartedEvent is published, this bean will receive it without fail. Currently the onApplicationEvent does not do anything apart from shouting to the world that it has received the event. But we can do pretty much anything here—like starting a brand new component, creating resource loaders, sending an email, and so on.

Now that we have our event listener, the next step is to bind the listener to the context. We do this by declaring the bean in our config file as shown here:

```
<bean name="contextStartEventListener"
  class="com.madhusudhan.jscore.containers.event.ContextStartedEventListener"/>
```

Once the context is started, the listener will receive a start event as expected.

Spring context publishes the following types of events:

ContextStartedEvent

> This event is published when the ApplicationContext is started. All beans receive a start signal once the ApplicationContext is started. The activities such as polling to database or observing a file system can be started once we receive this type of event.

ContextStoppedEvent

> This is the opposite of the start event. This event is published when the ApplicationContext is stopped. Our bean receives a stop signal from the framework so we can do housekeeping on the bean.

ContextRefreshedEvent

> A refresh event is emitted when the context is either refreshed or initialized.

ContextClosedEvent

> This event occurs when the ApplicationContext is closed. From closed state, a context *cannot* be restarted or refreshed.

RequestHandledEvent

> This is a web-specific event informing the receivers that a web request has been received.

For completeness, run the following client program which should start, stop, and refresh the context:

```
public class ContextEventListenerClient {
  private ConfigurableApplicationContext ctx = null;
  public void test() {
    ctx = new ClassPathXmlApplicationContext("containers-events-beans.xml");
    ctx.start();
    ctx.refresh();
    ctx.stop();
  }
  public static void main(String args[]) {
    ContextEventListenerClient client = new ContextEventListenerClient();
    client.test();
  }
}
```

Our listener will receive the appropriate events.

Publishing Custom Events

It's a fairly simple task to publish custom events. Let's suppose we want to publish an event whenever we receive a file larger than 100Mb.

In order to prepare our application for publishing custom events, we need four code structures to develop: The publisher, the listener, the event, and the client. Let's develop all of them here.

First we have to create an event by extending the ApplicationEvent—as our HugeFi
leEvent shown here:

```
public class HugeFileEvent extends ApplicationEvent {
  private String fileName = null;
  public HugeFileEvent(Object source, String fileName) {
    super(source);
    this.fileName = fileName;
  }
}
```

As mentioned earlier, the event class must extend the ApplicationEvent class.

Now, we need to create a publisher—HugeFileEventPublisher in this case. This class
implements Framework's ApplicationEventPublisherAware interface so it can be injected with a ApplicationEventPublisher object by calling the setApplicationEvent
Publisher method. The ApplicationEventPublisher has one method—publishE
vent—which is used to publish events.

```
public class HugeFileEventPublisher implements ApplicationEventPublisherAware{
  private ApplicationEventPublisher pub = null;

  public void setApplicationEventPublisher(ApplicationEventPublisher pub) {
    this.applicationEventPublisher = pub;
  }

  public void publish(String fileName){
    System.out.println("Publishing a HugeFileEvent, file is: "+fileName);
    HugeFileEvent hugeFileEvent = new HugeFileEvent(this,fileName);
    pub.publishEvent(hugeFileEvent);
  }
}
```

The third piece of code is our listener—no point in publishing events if there is no
listener (a bit like one-sided love!). We have already seen the implementation of a listener
in our earlier section—here's the HugeFileEventListener code shown for completeness:

```
public class HugeFileEventListener implements
  ApplicationListener<HugeFileEvent> {
  public void onApplicationEvent(HugeFileEvent event) {
    System.out.println("Received Event:"+event.getSource());
  }
}
```

Now that we have the basic classes in place, all we need is to wire them up and call them
from a client. We need to declare the publisher and listener beans as shown in the
following snippet:

```
<bean name="hugeFileEventPublisher"
  class="com.madhusudhan.jscore.containers.event.publish.HugeFileEventPublisher"/>
```

```
<bean name="hugeFileEventListener"
  class="com.madhusudhan.jscore.containers.event.publish.HugeFileEventListener"/>
```

Let's create a test client to make these code pieces work for us:

```
public class HugeFileEventClient {
  private ApplicationContext ctx = null;
  private HugeFileEventPublisher hugeFileEventPublisher = null;

  public void test() {
    ctx = new ClassPathXmlApplicationContext("containers-events-publish-beans.xml");
    hugeFileEventPublisher =
      ctx.getBean("hugeFileEventPublisher", HugeFileEventPublisher.class);
    hugeFileEventPublisher.publish("huge-file.txt");
  }
  public static void main(String args[]) {
    HugeFileEventClient client = new HugeFileEventClient();
    client.test();
  }
}
```

Once the context is created, fetch the publisher bean and invoke the publish method to publish an event. The event is created in the publish and is sent to the context. The listener then gets this event (framework delivers the event to all the context listeners) and invokes the appropriate processing.

Event Model Is Single Threaded

One important thing to keep in mind when working with Spring events handling is that Spring's event handling is *single threaded*—it is primarily synchronous in nature. That is, if an event is published, until and unless all the receivers get the message, the processes are blocked and the flow will not continue. If you have multiple listeners listening for an event, this single-thread model may hamper the performance of the application. Hence, care should be taken when designing your application if event handling is to be used.

Personally I would not depend on Spring's Events as it is not only single threaded but also locks us to the framework. You have to implement the framework's interfaces, thus making it worse when you wish to implement other frameworks in the future. There are plenty of open source alternatives such as EventBus (*http://eventbus.org*), Event Listener Framework (elf), or even Spring's Integration (although I admit Spring's Integration or JMS might be overkill for such a simple event mechanism).

See my other book *Just Spring Integration* if you're interested in learning Spring's Integration.

Autowiring

When creating a bean, we used to set the properties of the bean by using either `proper ty` or `constructor-arg` attributes. However, to save us typing, Spring has a sophisticated concept of *autowiring* these relationships and dependencies. This means that you don't have to explicitly mention the properties and their values, but setting the autowire property to a specfic value allows the framework to wire them with appropriate properties. This mechanism is called *autowiring*.

By default, there is no autowiring enabled (the same as setting the autowire attribute to "no"). Also, note that autowiring works only for references—the normal Java primities and Strings cannot be set using autowiring.

There are fundamentally three variations of autowiring, by name, by type, by constructor, as explained in the following sections—four if you consider mixing autowiring and explicit wiring!

Autowiring byName

When autowiring `byName` is enabled, the framework tries injecting the dependencies by matching the names to the property fields.

This is easily understood by an example. Let's say we have a `TradeReceiver` bean which has two properties—named as `tradePersistor` and `tradeTransformer` beans. When we choose the autowiring mechanism to be `byName`, Framework will locate these dependednt beans (as long as they are named exactly as the `TradeReceiver`'s properties) from the context and inject into the `TradeReceiver` bean.

First, here's the definition of the `TradeReceiver` class here:

```
public class TradeReceiver {
  private TradePersistor tradePersistor = null;
  private TradeTransformer tradeTransformer = null;
  ...
}
```

Our usual way is to define all three beans in the XML config file, then pass the references of persistor and transformer to `TradeReceiver`. However, with autowiring, you don't have to go this far.

In order to enable autowiring `byName`, we need to set the attribute `autowire` to `byName` on the bean in the config:

```
<bean name="tradeReceiver"
  class="com.madhusudhan.jscore.containers.autowire.TradeReceiver"
  autowire="byName"/>

<bean name="tradePersistor"
  class="com.madhusudhan.jscore.containers.autowire.TradePersistor"/>
```

```
<bean name="tradeTransformer"
    class="com.madhusudhan.jscore.containers.autowire.TradeTransformer"/>
```

In addition to this, we have defined the tradePersistor and tradeTransformer beans
in the config too.

Did you notice we did not define any properties such as tradePersistor or trade
Transformer on the tradeReceiver bean? We would have normally set these properties
by declaring them explicitly as shown here:

```
<bean name="tradeReceiver"
    class="com.madhusudhan.jscore.containers.autowire.TradeReceiver">
    <property name="tradePersistor" ref="tradePersistor"/>
    <property name="tradeTransformer" ref="tradeTransformer"/>
</bean>
```

How does this work then? Well, the attribute autowire="byName" does the magic for
us behind the scenes. This setting instructs the container to look for two properties with
the same names as tradeReceiver's variable names (tradePersistor and tradeTrans
former in this case). The container looks at all the beans instantiated and tries to match
them with the beans with the variable names of tradeReceiver. If matches are found,
it will inject those beans straightaway. Otherwise, it will throw exceptions thus notifying
the bean creation issues. Note that the autowiring principle works for only references.
You have to mix and match the autowiring and explicit wiring (hold on, we will look at
mixing these wiring types in couple of minutes).

Autowiring byType

Similar to byName, we need to set the autowire property to byType in order to enable
this type of autowiring. In this case, instead of looking for a bean with the same names,
the container searches for the *same types*. Taking the same example of TradeReceiver,
setting the autowire="byType" tells the container that it should look for a bean of type
TradePersistor and another one with a type of TradeTransformer.

```
<bean name="tradeReceiver"
    class="com.madhusudhan.jscore.containers.autowire.TradeReceiver"
    autowire="byType"/>
```

If the container finds the appropriate types, it will inject them into the bean. In the
above case, framework looks for two types, com.madhusudhan.jscore.containers.au
towire.TradePersis
tor and com.madhusudhan.jscore.containers.autowire.TradeTransformer in the
config file. If it finds them, they will be injected into the tradeReceiver bean. However,
if it finds more than one bean with the same type defined in the config, a fatal exception
is thrown.

Autowiring by constructor

It's not that hard to guess about our next autowiring counterpart—autowiring by constructor. This is similar to byType but applies to bean's constructor arguments only. As the name suggests, the constructor argument will be satisfied by searching for that type in the context. That is, if a bean has a constructor that takes an argument of another bean type, the container looks for that reference and injects it.

For example, we define a TradePersistor class with a single constructor that takes a datasource object:

```
public class TradePersistor {
  public TradePersistor (DataSource datasource){ ..}
}
```

If we enable autowiring by constructor, the container looks for an object of the type DataSource and injects it into the TradePersistor bean. You enable autowiring by constructor as shown here:

```
<bean name="tradePersistor"
  class="com.madhusudhan.jscore.containers.autowire.TradePersitor"
  autowire="constructor"/>
```

Mixing Autowiring with Explicit Wiring

We can get the best of both worlds by using autowiring and explicit wiring. Any ambiguities encountered while autowiring can be dealt with using explicit wiring.

For example, in the following snippet, the tradeReceiver is injected with two beans—the tradePersitor injected explicitly using our good old way, while the tradeTransformer is wired automatically using a byName variation.

```
<bean name="tradeReceiver"
  class="com.madhusudhan.jscore.containers.autowire.TradeReceiver"
  autowire="byName">
  <!-- The tradePersistor is set traditionally -->
  <property name="tradePersistor" ref="tradePersistor"/>
</bean>

<bean name="tradePersistor"
  class="com.madhusudhan.jscore.containers.autowire.TradePersistor"/>
<bean name="tradeTransformer"
  class="com.madhusudhan.jscore.containers.autowire.TradeTransformer"/>
```

We can also switch off autowiring for specific beans should we wish to do so. All we need to do is to set autowire-candidate to false on the bean definition—see here for an example—the tradePersistor is not interested in participating in autowiring mode:

```
<bean name="tradePersistor"
  class="com.madhusudhan.jscore.containers.autowire.TradePersistor"
  autowire-candidate="false"/>
```

Although autowiring saves us from writing extra metadata declarations, personally I wouldn't go for it. I prefer the explicit wiring style—less ambiguity and more readability.

Summary

This chapter completes our journey into core Spring. It explains the fundamentals of containers and their usage. It then delves into using autowiring beans where you do not have to set properties on the beans. It then explains various ways of instantiating the beans, such as static methods or factory methods. We have also seen event handling supported by the framework.

One of the important aspect of Spring is its support for enterprise features such as Spring JMS and Database. The next chapter explains the simplification Spring has brought into the Java messaging world.

CHAPTER 4

Advanced Concepts

The Spring framework comes with lots of bells and whistles. There are at times we wish to inject Java Collections such as Maps or Lists. There are also instances we wish to alter the bean configurations for our own customizations . Configuring such collections outside of the application in a properties file or customizing the beans to our own needs is easily done in Spring. While we learned the basics in the first three chapters, we discuss the more mature and advanced concepts in this chapter.

Bean Scopes

Did you wonder how many instances will be created when the Spring's container is loads up the bean config file during the application startup? Do we get the same instance whenever you query the container for the same bean? If we have a case where one and only one bean (such as a service or a factory) is to be created irrespective of the number of times you call the container, how is this achieved? Or for every call, how can we fetch a brand new instance? How does Spring achieve this?

Well, it turns out to be a simple config tag that dictates these types—the `scope` tag with values of `singleton` and `prototype`.

Singleton Scope

When you need one and only one instance of a bean (`TrainFactory` in this case), you should set the `scope` tag to `singleton`, as shown here:

```
<bean name="trainFactory" scope="singleton"
    class="com.madhusudhan.jscore.fundamentals.scope.TrainFactory">
</bean>
```

However, the default `scope` is *always* singleton. Hence, you can ignore the setting of `scope` to `singleton` as shown here:

```
<bean name="trainFactory"
    class="com.madhusudhan.jscore.fundamentals.scope.TrainFactory">
</bean>
```

Every time a `trainFactory` is injected into another bean or queried using the `getBean()` method, the same instance is returned.

Note that there is a subtle difference between the instance obtained using the Java Singleton pattern and Spring Singleton. Spring Singleton is a singleton per context or container, whereas the Java Singleton is per process and per class loader.

Prototype Scope

Prototype scope creates a new instance every time a call is made to fetch the bean. For example, we define a `Train` object that gets created every time it gets instantiated.

Because our requirement is to create a new `Train` everytime, the `scope` has to be set to `prototype` in our config file. Spring would then create a new `Train` object for every invocation.

```
<bean name="train"
  scope="prototype"
  class="com.madhusudhan.jscore.fundamentals.scope.Train">
  <property name="trainName" value="London to Paris Special"/>
</bean>
```

As you may have observed, nothing in the class definitions would indicate the scope of the classes. There seems to be no difference in the code base, whether using `single ton` or `prototype`. The scope is managed declaratively, hence giving you the option of turning it on or off according to the requirement.

For completeness, let's execute a test class that prints out the `Train` and `TrainFactory`'s hashCode values. The following is the test client:

```
public class TrainClient {
  private static ApplicationContext context = null;
  private Train train = null;
  private TrainFactory trainFactory = null;

  public void init() {
    context = new ClassPathXmlApplicationContext("fundamentals-beans.xml");
  }

  private void checkTrainInstance() {
    for (int i = 0; i < 10; i++) {
    train = context.getBean("train", Train.class);
          System.out.println("Train instance: " + train.getInstance());
    }
  }

  private void checkTrainFactoryInstance() {
```

```
    for (int i = 0; i < 10; i++) {
      trainFactory = context.getBean("trainFactory", TrainFactory.class);
      System.out.println("TrainFactory instance: " + trainFactory.getInstance());
    }
  }

  public static void main(String[] args) {
    TrainClient client = new TrainClient();
    client.init();
    client.checkTrainInstance();
    client.checkTrainFactoryInstance();
  }
}
```

We loop through 10 times to check the instance's hashCode value—obviously we expect the same hashCode for singleton and different hashCode for prototype beans. When the test is executed, the output is:

```
Train instance: 1443639316
Train instance: 975740206
Train instance: 1080513750
...
TrainFactory instance: 2074631480
TrainFactory instance: 2074631480
TrainFactory instance: 2074631480
...
```

As you can see the Train instance is different everytime while the TrainFactory is the same.

There are other types of scopes such as session, request, and global-session—they are used in the Spring's web applications.

Property Files

When defining the FileReader or FtpReader, for example, we have set the hard-coded properties in the XML file. The filename or the ftp hostname/credentials were all hard wired which is definitely not a good thing.

If we need to change the properties from one environment to another, we will have to modify this XML file. This is definitely not a good practice. Spring gives us another way of injecting these properties.

What we need to do is to define a property file with name-value pairs and let Spring's PropertyPlaceholderConfigurer read it. This class loads up a properties file specified by a location and resolves the properties.

Let's see how we can achieve this.

Create a JobSearchAgent class with two properties—location and type. The location attribute indicates the candidate's preferred job location while the type attribute indicates the type of job to search (permanent, temporary, etc.).

```
public class JobSearchAgent {
   private String location = null;
   private String type = null;
   // Setters and Getters for these properties
   // ...
}
```

We want these two properties to be loaded from an external properties file—the rational being that each candidate may have an associaed agent with him/her. So, the next step is to create a property file called fundamentals-beans.properties in our resources area and add the following properties and their values:

```
job.location = /users/mkonda/dev/js;
job.type = permanent;
```

Did you notice the convention that I'm following when naming the properties file? Usually, I prefer naming the properties file exactly as the bean definitions file except the extension (.properties in the former case).

The last bit of the puzzle is the config meta data of the JobSearchAgent class.

Edit the *fundamentals-beans.xml* file to add the framework's class named PropertyPla ceholderConfigurer. This class has a property called location, which should be pointing to our properties file:

```
<bean
 class="org.springframework.beans.factory.config.PropertyPlaceholderConfigurer">
   <property name="location" value="classpath:fundamentals-beans.properties"/>
</bean>
```

The PropertyPlaceholderConfigurer is a central class in resolving the properties. The responsibility of this PropertyPlaceholderConfigurer is to search for the property files in the classpath and load them into the application.

The last step is to parameterize the JobSearchAgent class's properties in the config file:

```
<bean name="jobSearchAgent"
     class="com.madhusudhan.jscore.fundamentals.properties.JobSearchAgent">
   <property name="type" value="${job.type}"/>
   <property name="location" value="${job.location}"/>
</bean>
```

The ${job.type} and ${job.location} properties resolves to the name-value pairs defined in the fundamentals-beans.properties. They are replaced appropriately during the runtime of the application thus allowing us to create environment-specific properties.

The format of the property attributes follow the famous Ant style—${name}. However, Framework provides a way of customizing the prefix and suffixes.

For example, if we want to call the properties as #[name] instead of following the default ${} style, we need to set two properties placeholderPrefix and placeholderSuffix with our choice. See the following snippet for an example:

```
<bean
  class="org.springframework.beans.factory.config.PropertyPlaceholderConfigurer">
    <property name="location" value="classpath:fundamentals-beans.properties"/>
    <property name="placeholderPrefix" value="#["/>
    <property name="placeholderSuffix" value="]"/>
</bean>
```

Of course, the bean properties should reflect these changes—see the values in bold:

```
<bean name="jobSearchAgent"
    class="com.madhusudhan.jscore.fundamentals.properties.JobSearchAgent">
    <property name="type" value="#[job.type]"/>
    <property name="location" value="#[job.location]"/>
</bean>
```

Should you wish to read properties from multiple locations, set the locations property with the list of property files as shown here:

```
<bean
  class="org.springframework.beans.factory.config.PropertyPlaceholderConfigurer">
    <property name="locations">
      <list>
        <value>classpath:fundamentals-beans.properties</value>
        <value>classpath:fundamentals-beans_1.properties</value>
      </list>
    </property>
</bean>
```

Property Editors

When we set the property values in the Spring config file, from the declaration, it sounds like the properties were just Strings or Java primitives. However, there will be instances when we need to pass in an externally initialized collection, object references, or other values. Spring follows the Java Bean style property editor mechanism to facilitate such requirements. We can inject any Java Collection such as List, Set, Map by declaring them in the config XML file. We can also provide java.util.Properties. We'll see them in action here.

If the property is another bean reference (a dependency), the actual type of the bean is resolved when injecting the dependency.

Injecting Java Collections

Injecting an initialized collection such as a List, Set, or Map couldn't be any easier in Spring. There is a specific syntax to follow in the config file so the collection is initialized before injecting.

Using lists, sets and maps

Lists are one of the frequent collections used heavily in Java programs. We may have instances of creating a pre-populated lists such as list of currencies, list of countries or list of week days, and so on.

The following CapitalCitiesManager class defines a variable called countriesList which holds the list of Countries as Strings. Obviously this is a static list that can be initialized outside the program in the config XML.

```
public class CapitalCitiesManager {
  private List<String> countriesList = null;

  // getters and setters
  public List<String> getCountriesList() {
    return countriesList;
  }
  public void setCountriesList(List<String> countriesList) {
    this.countriesList = countriesList;
  }
}
```

In order to use Lists, declare the property countryList (the property name should match to the variable name) with a list element. This list element will then hold individual value tags enclosing the values.

The following config metadata shows the usage of java.util.List in our CapitalCitiesManager class.

```
<bean name="capitalCitiesManager"
 class="com.madhusudhan.jscore.fundamentals.propertyeditor.CapitalCitiesManager">
  <property name="countriesList">
    <list>
      <value>United Kingdom</value>
      <value>United States Of America</value>
      <value>India</value>
      <value>Japan</value>
    </list>
  </property>
</bean>
```

Similarly, if you have to create list of countries by using a Set (remember, java.util.Set will not accept duplicates) values, swap the list tag shown in the above snippet with this set tag:

```
<bean name="capitalCitiesManager"
 class="com.madhusudhan.jscore.fundamentals.propertyeditor.CapitalCitiesManager">
  <property name="countriesSet">
  <set>
    <value>United Kingdom</value>
    <value>United Kingdom</value>
    <value>United States Of America</value>
    <value>United States Of America</value>
    <value>India</value>
    <value>Japan</value>
  </set>
</property>
```

Purposely, I have created the duplicate values for the above Set element. When you run the test client, you will see the Set populated with four unique countries!

Coming to Maps, as expected, we need to use the java.util.Map implementation as shown in the following code snippet:

```
public class CapitalCitiesManager {
  private Map<String,String> countriesCapitalsMap = null;

  //Getters and Setters
  public Map<String, String> getCountriesCapitalsMap() {
    return countriesCapitalsMap;
  }
  public void setCountriesCapitalsMap(Map<String, String> countriesCapitalsMap) {
    this.countriesCapitalsMap = countriesCapitalsMap;
  }
}
```

However, when configuring Maps, there are certain subtle differences. The element in a map is made of an Entry node, which has name-value pairs defined as key and value attributes:

```
<bean name="capitalCitiesManager"
 class="com.madhusudhan.jscore.fundamentals.propertyeditor.CapitalCitiesManager">
  <property name="countriesCapitalsMap">
    <map>
      <entry key="England" value="London"/>
      <entry key="USA" value="Washington DC"/>
    </map>
  </property>
</bean>
```

Values can also refer to any other object references—for example, the entry UK has a reference to UnitedKingdomUnion bean. See the snippet here here:

```
<bean name="capitalCitiesManager" class=
 "com.madhusudhan.jscore.fundamentals.propertyeditor.CapitalCitiesManager">
  <property name="countriesCapitalsRefMap">
    <map>
      <entry key="UK" value-ref="ukUnion"/>
```

```
      </map>
    </property>
  </bean>

  <bean name="ukUnion"
    class="com.madhusudhan.jscore.fundamentals.propertyeditor.UnitedKingdomUnion"/>
```

Note that the ukUnion bean is referenced using the `value-ref` tag instead of `value` tag as we did in the earlier snippet.

Injecting Java Properties

The `java.util.Properties` object represents a name-value pair. The following code snippet defines the `Properties` object in our `CapitalCitiesManager` class:

```
public class CapitalCitiesManager {
  private Properties countryProperties = null;
  public Properties getCountryProperties() {
    return countryProperties;
  }
  public void setCountryProperties(Properties countryProperties) {
    this.countryProperties = countryProperties;
  }
}
```

The next step is wiring up the bean in the config. The `countriesProperties` variable should be declared as a property to the bean.

See the XML config here:

```
  <bean name="capitalCitiesManager"
    class="com.madhusudhan.jscore.fundamentals.propertyeditor.CapitalCitiesManager">
    <property name="countryProperties">
      <props>
        <prop key="UK">London</prop>
        <prop key="USA">Washington DC</prop>
      </props>
    </property>
  </bean>
```

The `Properties` object is represented by `props` element as you can see above. Each of the element in the `Properties` has a `prop` attribute that will have our key and values.

Bean Post Processors

Spring allows us to poke into the bean's life cycle by implementing bean post processors. In these post processors, we get a chance to alter the configuration, set a custom value, or implement sophisticated `init` processes.

The Framework provides a `BeanPostProcessor` interface which is used to exploit this functionality. This interface has two callback methods: `postProcessBeforeInitiali` zation and `postProcessAfterInitialization`. The `BeanPostProcessor` is set per container only—all the beans in that container will be processed by this post processor. We can have multiple post processors doing various bits if we like.

As the names indicate, the `postProcessBeforeInitialization` method is invoked just before calling your `init-method` or `afterPropertiesSet` method on the bean. Our bean is just about to be implemented, but we have been given a chance to do something before the final call! Similarly, the `postProcessAfterInitialization` method is called just after the initialization of the bean is completed.

Let's take a simple case—any bean declared in a particular container should have a pre-set variable `componentName`. If the `componentName` is not set (is empty), then the bean should be set with a default value, say, `LONDON-DEFAULT-COMP`. The easiest way to achieve this requirement is to create a class that implements the `BeanPostProcessor` interface and modify the value of `componentName` variable.

First, we'll create a processor, in this case we call it `DefaultComponentNamePostProcessor`:

```
public class DefaultComponentNamePostProcessor implements BeanPostProcessor{
  public Object postProcessBeforeInitialization(Object o, String string)
  throws BeansException {
    System.out.println("PostProcess BEFORE init: " +o);
    if(o instanceof PostProcessComponent){
      ((PostProcessComponent)o).setComponentName("LONDON-DEFAULT-COMP");
    }
   return o;
  }

  public Object postProcessAfterInitialization(Object o, String string)
  throws BeansException {
    System.out.println("PostProcess AFTER init: " +o);
      if(o instanceof PostProcessComponent){
        System.out.println("Default Property:
    "+((PostProcessComponent)o).getComponentName());
      }
    return o;
  }
}
```

As you can see, the `DefaultComponentNamePostProcessor` class implements two superclass's methods (highlighted in bold). Any bean that's been created in this container will be processed by this post processor. What we are doing here is setting a property `componentName` during the `postProcessBeforeInitialization` method invocation while simply printing it out during the `postProcessAfterInitialization` method (and returning the unmodified instance).

To complete our discussion, we need to create a simple POJO `PostProcessComponent` that has a variable named `componentName` which will not be set yet.

Here's the code snippet of `PostProcessComponent` class:

```
public class PostProcessComponent {
  private String componentName = null;
  public String getComponentName() {
    return componentName;
  }
  public void setComponentName(String componentName) {
    this.componentName = componentName;
  }
}
```

The last thing we need to do is to declare the post processor and the bean in the XML config file:

```
<bean name="compNamePostProcessor"
  class="com...containers.postprocessor.DefaultComponentNamePostProcessor"/>
<bean name="postProcessComponent"
  class="com.madhusudhan.jscore.containers.postprocessor.PostProcessComponent"/>
```

We do not have to define the bean as a post processor anywhere in the config, just declare them as normal beans. The container will automatically find all the post processors and load them for further work.

When you run the example, you can see the following output:

```
PostProcess BEFORE init: PostProcessComponent{componentName=null}
PostProcess AFTER init: PostProcessComponent{componentName=LONDON-DEFAULT-COMP}
```

If you have several beans defined in the container config file with `componentName` not set, all of them will then be pre-proceessed by the `DefaultComponentNamePostProces sor` to set a default `componentName`.

We need to tell the framework that we're using post processors. If the container is `BeanFactory`, we have to invoke `addBeanPostProcessor` (our processor) on the `Bean Factory` in order to set the post processor instance.

However, if `ApplicationContext` is our container, defining the post processor in the config file is adequate. The container automatically looks at the class to see if it's a post processor and then invokes the appropriate methods during the instantiation of the bean.

Note that the `BeanPostProcessors` are applied per container while the bean `init` or `destroy` methods are applied per bean.

Parent-Child Bean Definitions

Spring allows us to declare abstract and implemented classes in the configuration. If AbstractKlass is an abstract class and Klass is a sub-class of it, they can be configured as shown here:

```
<bean name="abstractKlass"
  class="com.madhusudhan.jscore.fundamentals.inherit.AbstractKlass"
  abstract="true"/>
<bean name="klass"
  class="com.madhusudhan.jscore.fundamentals.inherit.Klass"
  parent="abstractKlass"/>
```

When we declare an abstract class, we need decorate it with abstract="true" as shown in bold in the above snippet. The subclass should be defined with parent attribute refering to this abstract class.

Summary

This chapter completes our journey into core Spring. It explains the fundamentals of containers and their usage. It then delves into using autowiring beans where you do not have to set properties on the beans. It then explains various ways of instantiating the beans, such as static methods or factory methods. We have also seen event handling supported by the framework.

One important aspect of Spring is its support for enterprise features such as Spring JMS and Database. The next chapter explains the simplification Spring has brought into the Java messaging world.

CHAPTER 5

Spring JMS

The Java Messaging Service (JMS) API, which came into existence a decade ago, was an instant hit in the area of distributed messaging and enterprise applications. The demand for easier and standardized integration with the Messaging Middleware was the drive for creating this technology. Although the API is straightforward and relatively easy, Spring has taken a step forward in creating an even easier framework around it. This chapter will introduce you to the JMS basics and explains Spring's take on JMS and how it simplified developers' lives even further.

Two-Minute JMS

JMS provides a mechanism of communication between applications without being coupled. The applications can talk to each other via the JMS provider without even knowing who is on the other side of the fence.

For example, a `PriceQuote` service can publish price quotes onto a channel, expecting *someone* to receive them. However, the service may not be aware of any consumers that would consume these quotes. Similarly, the consumers may not have any clue about the source of the data or the producers. In a way, they are hidden behind the walls, just interacting via destinations or channels. Producers and consumers don't have to bother about each other's existence as long as they know their expected messages are delivered or received, respectively.

There are three important moving pieces in JMS: the *service provider*, the *producer*, and the *consumer*.

The service provider is the central piece, while the other two are either data producers or consumers. The architecture is based on hub and spoke; that is, the server maintains a central ground like a hub while producers and consumers act like the spokes.

The overall responsibility in this architecture is taken by the service provider. The provider makes sure all the consumers receive the messages, while at the same time, all producers are able to publish the messages. I would recommend picking up a book on the subject to understand JMS in detail.

Messaging Models

In JMS, there are primarily two messaging models: one is *point-to-point* (or P2P, as it is sometimes called) and the other is *publish-subscribe* (Pub/Sub). There are specific use cases where you should use these models. Although both differ fundamentally in delivery and reception mechanisms, a unified API is used to access both the models.

Point-to-point messaging

In point-to-point (P2P) mode, a message is delivered to a *single* consumer via a destination—it's for a specific consumer only. A publisher publishes a message onto a destination, while a consumer consumes the message off that destination. This is analogous to a birthday greeting card sent to you—only to you!

When a message is published in P2P mode to a queue, *one and only one* consumer can receive that message. Even if there are hundreds of consumers connected to that queue, still only one consumer will get that message delivered. Of course, you never know who's the lucky winner though!

The destination in a point-to-point model is called a Queue.

Pub/sub messaging

On the other hand, if a message is published to a destination, there could be several subscribers each receiving a *copy* of the message. The publisher obviously publishes the message once. All the subscribers interested will head to the same destination to consume that message. The JMS Provider makes sure each of the subscribers receives a copy of the message. This is analogous to a car dealer sending offers to you and possibly thousands of others!

The destination in a Pub/Sub model is called a Topic.

Spring JMS

The Spring framework has simplified the JMS API quite a bit. All we need to do is follow a simple *template* software pattern in order to understand the Spring JMS usage. Before we go into code examples, let me explain the high-level classes and their usage.

The core of Spring JMS revolves around a single class, JmsTemplate. If you understand this one class in the Spring JMS framework, you are good to go! The JmsTemplate class is heavily used in Spring JMS for both message consumption and production. The only case `JmsTemplate` is not used is for asynchronous message consumption. We will discuss this case a bit later in the chapter.

First, let's start digging into the `JmsTemplate` class.

Mother of All: The JmsTemplate Class

We can use the `JmsTemplate` class for both publishing and consuming the messages. The template class hides all the plumbing needed for connecting to a provider. It also abstracts away lots of boilerplate code for publishing or receiving the messages. It manges the resources, such as connections, behind the scenes.

When using Spring JMS, the usual way is to configure a `JmsTemplate` instance (similar to a normal bean) and inject into our bean. We can set some Qualitiy of Service (QOS) properties such as priority, and delivery mode on the class, but the `ConnectionFacto ry` property is mandatory. The `ConnectionProperty` provides the enough information about the service provider to connect to it. There are other properties that are required for more features (such as `defaultDestination` and `receiveTimeout` parameters), which we will see in the following sections.

The template works by using callsbacks—callbacks such as `MessageCreator` for the message creation, `SessionCallback` for associating with a `Session`, and `ProducerCall back` for creating a message producer.

Once configured and instantiated, the `JmsTemplate` instance is thread-safe, so it can be shared across different beans without having to worry about session corruption.

There are primarily two ways of creating or instantiating `JmsTemplate`. One is to create the class by using a normal new operator, while the other is to declare and configure it in a configuration file. Both of them require us to pass in a `ConnectionFactory` property, though.

The `TradePublisher` class, shown here, uses a `JmsTemplate` for its message publication. The JmsTemplate is instantiated by passing in the constuctor argument - a `connec tionFactory` instance.

```
public class TradePublisher {
  private String destinationName = "justspring.core.jms.trades";
  private JmsTemplate jmsTemplate = null;

  public void setConnectionFactory(ConnectionFactory connectionFactory) {
    // create the JmsTemplate using the injected ConnectionFactory
    jmsTemplate = new JmsTemplate(connectionFactory);
  }
  ...
}
```

Once we have the `TradePublisher` created with a `JmsTempate` instance, the next step is to use this instance to publish our messages. There is a send method on the `jmsTem` plate instance that we should invoke to publish a message. There are basically two variants of the send method—one that takes in a destination and another that doesn't —the MessageCreator callback is mandatory though. We'll go through them in a few minutes.

The following snippet shows the usage:

```
public class TradePublisher {
  // access the template when publishing the message
  public void publishTrade(final Trade t) {
    jmsTemplate.send(destinationName, new MessageCreator() {
    @Override
    public Message createMessage(Session session) throws JMSException {
      ObjectMessage msg = session.createObjectMessage();
      msg.setObject(t);
        return msg;
      }
    });
  }
}
```

The only requirement in this case is to wire the ConnectionFactory to the publisher in your config so it can be injected when the bean is created. Of course, you need to instantiate the JmsTemplate object, using this connection factory. Here's the XML file:

```
<bean name="tradePublisher"
  class="com.madhusudhan.jscore.jms.TradePublisher">
  <property name="connectionFactory" ref="connectionFactory"/>
</bean>

<bean id="connectionFactory"
  class="org.apache.activemq.ActiveMQConnectionFactory">
  <property name="brokerURL" value="tcp://localhost:61616" />
</bean>
```

As we discussed earlier, there is another way to get a hold of JmsTemplate in our bean. We can wire the template with a connection factory and inject into our bean—this is all done in the config. If you carefully observe, all we did was moving the creation of template from our application to the framework.

```
<bean name="tradePublisher" class="com.madhusudhan.jscore.jms.TradePublisher">
  <property name="jmsTemplate" ref="jmsTemplate"/>
</bean>
<bean id="jmsTemplate" class="org.springframework.jms.core.JmsTemplate">
  <property name="connectionFactory" ref="connectionFactory" />
</bean>
<bean id="connectionFactory" class=
  "org.apache.activemq.ActiveMQConnectionFactory">
  <property name="brokerURL" value="tcp://localhost:61616" />
</bean>
```

Your bean will have a reference to JmsTemplate via a setter method. The TradePublish er with a wired-in template as shown in the following snippet:

```
public class TradePublisher {
  private String destinationName = "justspring.core.jms.trades";
  private JmsTemplate jmsTemplate = null;

  public void setJmsTemplate(JmsTemplate jmsTemplate) {
    this.jmsTemplate = jmsTemplate;
  }

  public JmsTemplate getJmsTemplate() {
    return jmsTemplate;
  }

  public void publishTrade(final Trade t) {
    ...
  }
}
```

The JmsTemplate is injected into the related class that requires publishing or receiving messages from a JMS server, in this case the TradePublisher. As you can see, the ConnectionFactory is already wired to the JmsTemplate declaratively.

As we mentioned earlier, for sending messages, the JmsTemplate exposes these three methods:

```
send(MessageCreator msgCreator) //Default Destination

send(String destinationName, MessageCreator msgCreator)

send(Destination destinationName, MessageCreator msgCreator)
```

The first one assumes that messages should end up in a default destination, while the next two methods specify the destination. The MessageCreator argument is a callback hook so we can create the appropriate JMS Message. The callback has one method, createMessage(Session session). Using this session object, we create one of the types of Message with data.

Check out the publishTrade method implementation above in the TradePublisher class now to get a complete picture.

In the JMS world, all messages should be declared as one of the predefined five types before attempting to publish or receive them. The five types are TextMessage, Byte sMessage, ObjectMessage, StreamMessage, and MapMessage. You should consult the JMS API for the details of these messages.

Publishing Messages

Let's develop an example to understand the mechanics of message publication.

The StudentEnroller is the publishing component in the workflow that would be invoked whenever a Student enrolls for a course. The aim is to publish the enrolled Student onto a JMS destination so the parties interested will consume and act on them (probably to lure the student to take one of their subjects or to provide info about the library facilities, cafeteria, or unions).

The following snippet shows the code:

```
public class StudentEnroller {
  private String destinationName = null;
  private JmsTemplate jmsTemplate = null;

  public void publish(final Student s) {
    getJmsTemplate().send(getDestinationName(), new MessageCreator() {
      @Override
      public Message createMessage(Session session) throws JMSException {
        TextMessage m = session.createTextMessage();
        m.setText("Enrolled Student: " + s.toString());
        return m;
        }
      });
    }
  // setters and getters for the
  //jmsTemplate and destinationName variables
  ...
}
```

The StudentEnroller has two instance variables: jmsTemplate and destination Name. The JmsTemplate is used to publish the messages and the destinationName defines the location (queue or topic) where the messages should be sent.

The StudentEnroller instance is injected with a JmsTemplate instance and a destina tionName value at runtime. The publish method on the StudentEnroller instance is invoked when a client wishes to publish a Student message.

In order to create a JMS Message, we should use Spring's MessageCreator implementation. The template class expects a new instance of this callback with createMes sage() being implemented:

```
public Message createMessage(Session session) throws JMSException {
  TextMessage m = session.createTextMessage();
  m.setText("Enrolled Student: " + s.toString());
  return m;
}
```

The appropriate message is created using the session, in this case a TextMessage.

Before injecting the JmsTemplate into StudentEnroller, it is fully configured in the Spring's XML file. The template also has a variable called connectionFactory that needs to be defined and referenced. The connection factory is specific to individual JMS Providers. I am going to use ActiveMQ as the JMS Provider for the rest of the chapter, but you can use any other providers that are JMS-compliant (so the code should work without tweaking for each provider).

The ActiveMQ connection factory requires a `brokerUrl` property to be set as shown here:

```
<bean id="jmsTemplate" class="org.springframework.jms.core.JmsTemplate">
  <property name="connectionFactory" ref="connectionFactory" />
</bean>
<bean id="connectionFactory" class=
  "org.apache.activemq.ActiveMQConnectionFactory">
  <property name="brokerURL" value="tcp://localhost:61616"/>
</bean>
```

The last piece is the declaration of the `StudentEnroller` bean itself in the config file wired with the two properties `jmsTemplate` and `destinationName`.

```
<bean name="studentEnroller" class=
  "com.madhusudhan.jscore.jms.pub.StudentEnroller">
  <property name="destinationName" value="topic.STUDENTS"/>
  <property name="jmsTemplate" ref="jmsTemplate"/>
</bean>
```

Write a simple test client that creates a Spring container by loading the *jms-pub-beans.xml* config file.

```
public class StudentEnrollerClient {
  private ApplicationContext ctx = null;
  private StudentEnroller enroller = null;
  public StudentEnrollerClient() {
    ctx = new ClassPathXmlApplicationContext("jms-pub-beans.xml");
    enroller = (StudentEnroller) ctx.getBean("studentEnroller");
  }
  public void publishStudent(Student s) {
    System.out.println("Publishing Student..");
    enroller.publish(s);
  }
  public static void main(String[] args) {
    StudentEnrollerClient client = new StudentEnrollerClient();
    Student s = new Student();
    client.publishStudent(s);
  }
}
```

The client gets ahold of the `StudentEnroller` instance to invoke the publish method with a new `Student` object. The `StudentEnroller` was already injected with the dependencies such as `jmsTemplate` and `destinationName` (see the config declaration).

Now, run the ActiveMQ server. The server is started and running on our local machine (hence, localhost) on a default port 61616.

Run the client and if all is set correctly, we should see a message landing up in the ActiveMQ destination.

```
Publishing Student..
Successfully published student message to topic.STUDENTS
```

Note that the ActiveMQ creates the required destinations (in this case the topic.STU DENTS topic) on demand if they do not exist.

Sending Messages to Default Destination

If you wish to send the messages to a default destination, use the JmsTemplate's send(MessageCreator msgCreator) method variant. As the method signature suggests, it does not take any parameter for destination—the message is destined to go to a default destination. This default destination, however, needs to be wired in the config file.

In order to create a destination in the config file, we need to use a concrete implementation of javax.jms.Destination class—usually provided by the JMS providers. In the case of ActiveMQ, the destination is org.apache.activemq.command.ActiveMQTopic which is declared as a bean first here:

```
<bean id="defaultDestination" class="org.apache.activemq.command.ActiveMQTopic">
  <constructor-arg value="topic.DEFAULT_STUDENTS" />
</bean>
```

Then add a property defaultDestination in our JmsTemplate, making the reference point to the above destination:

```
<bean id="jmsTemplate" class="org.springframework.jms.core.JmsTemplate">
  <property name="connectionFactory" ref="connectionFactory" />
  <property name="defaultDestination" ref="defaultDestination" />
</bean>
```

Now that the moving parts are glued together, see the following publishing code snippet. Note that the send method does not have any reference to the destination.

```
public void publishToDefautDestination(final Student s) {
  getDefaultDestinationJmsTemplate().send(new MessageCreator() {
    @Override
    public Message createMessage(Session session) throws JMSException {
      ....
    }
  });
}
```

Declaring a Topic

By default, the JmsTemplate assumes that your messaging mode is point-to-point and hence the destination to be a Queue. However, if you wish to change this mode to pub/

sub, all you are required to do is wire in a property called `pubSubDomain`, setting it to true.

```
<bean id="jmsTemplate" class="org.springframework.jms.core.JmsTemplate">
  ...
  <property name="pubSubDomain" value="true" />
</bean>
```

This way, we are expecting the messages to be published onto to a `Topic`. Remember to create the queues or topic in the config as shown here (for ActiveMQ):

```
<!- Queue-->
<bean id="defaultDestination"
  class="org.apache.activemq.command.ActiveMQQueue">
  <constructor-arg value="queue.STUDENTS" />
</bean>

<!-- Topic -->
<bean id="defaultDestination"
  class="org.apache.activemq.command.ActiveMQTopic">
  <constructor-arg value="topic.STUDENTS" />
</bean>
```

Receiving Messages

Using `JmsTemplate` makes consuming the messages simple. However, a bit of complexity arises when the reception modes are considered. The two modes in which you can receive messages are *synchronous* and *asynchronous* modes.

In synchronous mode, we will not be able to process any other actions until and unless we receive at least one message from the server. The thread that calls the receive method will not return, but waits indefinitely to pick up the message. As this is more of a single-theaded nature, I recommend not use this mode unless you have a strong case. Should you have no alternatives other than using the synchronous receive method, use it at least by setting a timeout so the waiting thread can gracefully exit after the timeout.

In the asynchronous mode, the client will let the provider know that it would be interested in receiving the messages from a destination. When a message arrives at that given destination, the provider checks the list of clients interested in that message and sends the message to those list of clients.

We use `JmsTemplate`'s `receive` method to consume messages in this fashion.

Receiving Messages Synchronously

The receive method on the templace instance takes in a destination so it can start consuming from there. The `JobsReceiver` shown here connects to a JMS provider and tries to receive messages (the instance has been injected with a `JmsTemplate` object).

```
public class JobsReceiver {
  private JmsTemplate jmsTemplate = null;
  private String destinationName = null;

  public void receiveMessages() {
    Message msg = getJmsTemplate().receive(destinationName);
    System.out.println("Job Received: " + msg);
  }
  ...
}
```

The receive method waits until the destination holds at least a message. As explained earlier, the receive method is a blocking call, which may waste CPU cycles if no message exists in the queue. So, use the receiveTimeout variable with the appropriate value. The receiveTimeout is an attribute on JmsTemplate that needs to be declared in config file, which is shown here:

```
<bean id="jmsTemplate" class="org.springframework.jms.core.JmsTemplate">
  <property name="connectionFactory" ref="connectionFactory" />
  <property name="receiveTimeout" value="2000" />
  ...
</bean>
```

In the above snippet, the JobsReceiver will timeout after two seconds if it does not receive any messages in that time period.

We can also receive messages from a defaultDestination. As we did earlier, what we have to do is wire the jmsTemplate with a defaultDestination property. Simple!

```
<bean id="jmsTemplate" class="org.springframework.jms.core.JmsTemplate">
  <property name="defaultDestination" value="topic.DEFAULT_JOBS" />
  ...
</bean>
```

Receiving messages asynchronously is a bit different, let's see how we can do that.

Receiving Messages Asynchronously

In order to receive the messages asynchronously, we have to do a couple of things:

- Create a class that implements the MessageListener interface.
- Wire a Spring JMS Container in your spring beans XML file with a reference to your listener. We will talk about Containers in a minute.

So, the asynchronous client must implement JMS API's interface MessageListener. This interface has one method called onMessage that must be implemented by your class. The BookOrderMessageListener, for example, is a simple class that implements the MessageListener. The method does not do much except print out the message to the console.

```
public class BookOrderMessageListener implements MessageListener{
  @Override
  public void onMessage(Message msg) {
    System.out.println("Book order received:"+msg.toString());
  }
}
```

The second part is the task of wiring the containers.

Don't confuse these containers with the ApplicationContext or BeanFactory containers.

These containers are utility classes provided by the framework used in clients that are destined to receive messages. The containers are simple yet powerful classes that hide away all the complexities of connections and sessions. They are responsible for fetching the data from the JMS Provider and pushing it to your listener. They do this by having a reference to ConnectionFactory (and hence JMS Provider) and a reference to our listener class.

Now, let's looks at the workings in detail.

Wire up the container and the listener as shown in the following code snippet. Define an instance of DefaultMessageListenerContainer and inject it with a connectionFactory, destination, and messageListener instances.

Note that the messageListener class refers to our listener class.

```
<bean id="bookOrderListener"
  class="com.madhusudhan.jscore.jms.async.BookOrderMessageListener"/>

<bean id="defaultListenerContainer"
  class="org.springframework.jms.listener.DefaultMessageListenerContainer">
  <property name="connectionFactory" ref="connectionFactory" />
  <property name="destination" ref="defaultDestination" />
  <property name="messageListener" ref="bookOrderListener" />
</bean>
```

Once the wiring is done, fire up the client, which loads up the above beans. It would start up the messageListener instance, which waits to receive messages from the JMS server.

Publish a message onto the destination and we can see that message popping up at the messageListener client.

Spring Message Containers

We have seen the usage of DefaultMessageListenerContainer in the previous section. Spring provides three different types of containers for receiving messages asynchronously, including the DefaultMessageListenerContainer. The other two are Simple MessageListenerContainer and ServerSessionMessageListenerContainer.

The SimpleMessageListenerContainer is basically the simplest of all and is not recommended for production use. On the other hand, ServerSessionMessageListener Container is one level higher than DefaultMessageListenerContainer in complexity as well as features. This works if we want to work with JMS sessions directly. It is also used in the situation where XA transactions are required.

The DefaultMessageListenerContainer is well-suited for most of the applications and does allow you to participate in external transactions. Obviously choose the appropriate one based on your application's requirement.

Message Converters

One of the requirements when publishing a message is to convert your domain object into five predefined JMS message types. We cannot simply publish or receive domain objects such as Trade or Order, even if they are properly serialized Java Objects. So, if you wish to publish your domain objects, you need to convert them into the appropriate JMS Message type.

See the following publish method shown here:

```
public void publish(final Student s) {
  getJmsTemplate().send(getDestinationName(), new MessageCreator() {
    @Override
    public Message createMessage(Session session) throws JMSException {
      TextMessage m = session.createTextMessage();
      m.setText("Enrolled Student: " + s.toString());
      return m;
    }
  });
}
...
}
```

Did you notice that in order to send a message, we need to work with a session (to create appropriate object) and message creators (which provides us the session)? It's not that clean, is it?

The publish method can be enhanced to lose its wrinkles and look smart as shown—with the help of converters. See the enhanced method shown here:

```
public void publish(final Student student) {
  jmsTemplate.convertAndSend(destinationName, student);
}
```

The convertAndSend method will hide away all the extra boiler plate code. We can acheive this goal by using Spring's MessageConverters. They do the conversions easily without us having to sweat it anymore. Once the converter is plugged into the JmsTemplate, we do have to worry about the conversions. Of course, we have to write one of the converters to begin with though!

Let's see how the converters work.

First, we should create a class that implements the MessageConverter interface. This interface has two methods: fromMessage and toMesage methods. As the names indicate, we code these methods either to convert a JMS message to a domain object or vice versa.

The following code shows a typical converter used for Account objects:

```java
public class AccountConveter implements MessageConverter {
  @Override
  public Object fromMessage(Message msg) throws JMSException,
                            MessageConversionException {
    Account t = (Account) ((ObjectMessage) msg).getObject();
    System.out.println("fromMessage: " + msg.toString());
    return t;
  }

  @Override
  public Message toMessage(Object obj, Session session) throws JMSException,
                            MessageConversionException {
    ObjectMessage objMsg = session.createObjectMessage();
    objMsg.setObject((Account) obj);
    System.out.println("toMessage: " + objMsg.toString());
    return objMsg;
  }
}
```

In the fromMessage method, the Account object is grabbed from JMS ObjectMessage and converted to the actual domain object. Whereas, in the toMessage method, we use the passed-in session object to create an ObjectMessage and push the domain object by using setObject method.

Now that we have created an Account converter, the next step is to wire it into the JmsTemplate object.

```xml
<bean id="accountConverter"
  class="com.madhusudhan.jscore.jms.convert.AccountConverter"/>

<bean id="jmsTemplate" class="org.springframework.jms.core.JmsTemplate">
  <property name="messageConverter" ref="accountConverter"/>
  ....
</bean>
```

In the publisher and receiver code, you need to change the send and receive methods to convertAndSend() and receiveAndConvert() so the converter bean gets used at publishing and receiving end.

```java
//Publisher
public void publish(final Student student) {
  jmsTemplate.convertAndSend(destinationName, student);
}
```

```
//Receiver
public void receive() {
  Object o = jmsTemplate.receiveAndConvert(destinationName);
}
```

Whenever we publish an Account message, the jmsTemplate uses the converter to convert the Account to ObjectMessage. Similarly when receiving, the template calls the converter to do the reverse conversion. This way, you write the converter once and use it everywhere and at all times.

Summary

We have seen Java Messaging in action in this chapter. We briefly touched the subject of JMS and delved into using Spring's JmsTemplate class. We learned how we can publish our messages using the template class. We also saw how we can receive messages synchronously and asynchronously using Spring's framework classes called Message Containers. Lastly, we touched on the converters that would convert JMS message types to our business domain types and take away some more boilerplate code.

The next chapter deals with persistence and retrieval of Data, using Spring's JDBC and Hibernate support.

CHAPTER 6

Spring Data

Data persistence and retrieval are inevitable operations in an enterprise world. The advent of JDBC paved the way to interact with multiple databases with ease and comfort. JDBC techlogies have gained popularity in no time because of their unified API to access any database, be it MySQL or Oracle or Sybase or any Relational Database System.

Spring took one step ahead and created an even lighter framework, abstracting the JDBC behind the scenes. Although the JDBC and Spring marriage makes a happy family, there are some unsophisticated or unavailable features from the joint venture. One feature that comes to mind is the support for Object Relational mappings. We still have to write plain old SQL statements to access the data from persistent stores. This is the opportunity Hibernate grabbed and became an instant hit! With millions of downloads over the time, it is now a popular and powerful open source framework. Spring added more abstraction on top of the already powerful Hibernate to make it even better.

This chapter explains how the Spring Framework can be used effectively for accessing databases, without even having to worry about connections and statements. We then continue on to Spring's ORM support, using Hibernate.

JDBC and Hibernate

The joint venture did not attempt to bridge the gap between Objects and Relational Data. JDBC is certainly one of the first-hand choices for a Java developer when working with databases. JDBC abstracts away the intricacies involved in accessing different databases. It gives a clear and concise API to do the job easily.

As many developers who worked with JDBC will moan about, there is a lot of redundant or boilerplate code that needs to be written (or cut and pasted!), even if our intention is to fetch a single row of data.

The Spring Framework has changed this scenario drastically. Using a simple template pattern, Spring has revolutionized database access, digesting the boilerplate code altogether into itself. We do not have to worry about the unnecessary bootstrapping and resource management code or ugly exceptions. We are at last able to do what we have been employed to do—write just the business logic. We will see in this chapter how the framework has achieved this objective.

There is a second scenario to consider: we often wish to work with relational entities as if they are objects in your code. As relational entities differ from Java Objects, unless there is a bridge between them, this wish will not be fulfilled.

The good news that there are softwares built to manage this gap—simply called as Object Relational Mapping (ORM) frameworks. Hibernate, Java Data Objects (JDO), iBatis, and TopLink belong to this category. Using these ORM tools, we do not have to work at a low level as exposed by JDBC; instead we manipulate the data as objects.

For example, a table called MOVIES consists of many rows (Movies). The analogue to this relational entity would be modeled as a Movie object in our code, and the mapping of the MOVIE row to Movie domain object is performed by the framework behind the scenes.

Spring JDBC

We can agree that JDBC is a simple API for data access. However, when it comes to coding, it is still cumbersome, as we still have to write unnecessary, rudimentary code. Some say that about 80 percent of the code is repetitious. In a world of reusabiltiy, this is unacceptable. Spring does exactly this—abstracts away all the resource management so we can concentrate on the meat of the application. It might not surprise you to know that Spring "reuses" its template design pattern, allowing us to interact with the databases in a clean and easy manner. The core of the JDBC package revolves around one class: JdbcTemplate. This class plays the key role in accessing data from our components.

JdbcTemplate

The basic and most useful class from the framework is the JdbcTemplate. This call should serve to do most of your work. But should you require a bit more sophistication, the two variants of JdbcTemplate—the SimpleJdbcTemplate and NamedParameterJdbc Template—should provide you that.

The JdbcTemplate class provides the common aspects of database operations, such as inserting and updating data, using prepared statements, querying tables by using standard SQL queries, invoking stored procedures, and so on. It can also iterate over the ResultSet data efficiently and effectively.

The connection management is hidden from the user, and so is the resource pooling and exception management. Regarding the exceptions, one does not have to clutter the code with `try-catch` blocks because the database-specific exceptions are wrapped under covers by Spring's Runtime Exceptions.

As always inline with the template design pattern, the `JdbTemplate` provides callback interfaces for us to implement our business logic. For example, `PreparedStatement Callback` is used for creating `PreparedStatements`, while `RowCallbackHandler` is where you extract the `ResultSet` into your domain objects. The `CallableStatement Callback` is used when executing a stored procedure. We will work briefly with these callbacks in the next few sections.

Configuring JdbcTemplate

Before we can jump into working with the `JdbcTemplate`, we need to take care of a few details about its creation. First, we need to supply a `DataSource` to the `JdbcTemplate` so it can configure itself to get database access. As we have seen in the previous chapter (JMS), just as `ConnectionFactory` was the gateway to a JMS Provider, so is the `Data Source` the gateway to our Database. It supplies the connection information which is used by the JdbcTemplate to get access to the underlying databse.

You can configure the `DataSource` in the XML file as shown in the following code snippet. I am using an open source JDBC framework—*Apache commons DBCP*—for creating my datasources.

```
<bean id="movieDataSource" class="org.apache.commons.dbcp.BasicDataSource"
destroy-method="close">
  <property name="driverClassName" value="${jdbc.driver}"/>
  <property name="url" value="${jdbc.url}"/>
  <property name="username" value="${jdbc.username}"/>
  <property name="password" value="${jdbc.password}"/>
</bean>
```

Once we have the datasource created, our next job is to create the `JdbcTemplate`.

We have primarily two options: First, we can instantiate a `JdbcTemplate` in our Data Access Object (DAO), injecting the `DataSource` into it. Alternatively, we can define the `JdbcTemplate` in the XML file, wiring the datasource to it, and then injecting the `JdbcTemplate` reference into the DAO class. The following snippet uses this second option:

```
<bean id="jdbcTemplate" class="org.springframework.jdbc.core.JdbcTemplate">
  <property name="dataSource" ref="movieDataSource"/>
</bean>

<bean id="movieDataSource" class="org.apache.commons.dbcp.BasicDataSource"
  destroy-method="close">

  ....
</bean>
```

The JdbcTemplate is a threadsafe object once configured, so you can inject it into any number of DAOs.

Let's define the DAO for accessing the MOVIES database. The following snippet shows this class:

```
public class MovieDAO implements IMovieDAO {
  private JdbcTemplate jdbcTemplate = null;

  private void setJdbcTemplate(JdbcTemplate jdbcTemplate){
    this.jdbcTemplate = jdbcTemplate;
  }

  private JdbcTemplate getJdbcTemplate() {
    return this.jdbcTemplate;
  }
  ...
}
```

The IMovieDAO is the interface that has all the movie-related functionality which is shown here:

```
public interface IMovieDAO {
  public Movie getMovie(String id);
  public String getStars(String title);
  public List<Movie> getMovies(String sql);
  public List<Movie> getAllMovies();
  public void insertMovie(Movie m);
  public void updateMovie(Movie m);
  public void deleteMovie(String id);
  public void deleteAllMovies();
}
```

The MovieDAO has JdbcTemplate as a member variable. It is configured and wired with a datasource in the XML file and injected into our concrete DAO. The wiring XML file is shown here:

```
<bean id="movieDao" class="com.madhusudhan.jscore.data.MovieDAO">
  <property name="jdbcTemplate" ref="jdbcTemplate"/>
</bean>

<bean id="jdbcTemplate" class="org.springframework.jdbc.core.JdbcTemplate">
  <property name="dataSource" ref="movieDataSource"/>
</bean>

<bean id="movieDataSource" class="org.apache.commons.dbcp.BasicDataSource"
  destroy-method="close">
  ....
</bean>
```

Here is a snippet of the MovieDAO class.

```
public class MovieDAO implements IMovieDAO {
  private JdbcTemplate jdbcTemplate = null;

  private void setJdbcTemplate(JdbcTemplate jdbcTemplate){
    this.jdbcTemplate = jdbcTemplate;
  }

  private JdbcTemplate getJdbcTemplate() {
    return this.jdbcTemplate;
  }
  ...
}
```

That's it! Your JdbcTemplate is configured and ready to be used straightaway. Let's concentrate on what we can do with the template in our hand.

Using JdbcTemplate

The simplest operation is to fetch movie actors using a criteria such as a movie title. We can write a simple SQL query like select stars from MOVIES to retrieve the movie actors.

Our MovieDAO has a method getStars() that takes a title and returns comma-separated stars list. The snippet here shows the implementation of this query:

```
@Override
public String getStars(String title) {

  String stars = getJdbcTemplate().
    queryForObject("select stars from MOVIES where title='"+ title +"'",
              String.class);
  return stars;
}
```

The query was executed using queryForObject method on JdbcTemplate. This method takes two parameters, a SQL query without bind variables and an expected type of the result.

The expected result is a comma-separated stars list. We can improve this query by parameterizing the query. The where clause will have a bind variable that will change on queries. It is shown in the listing here:

```
@Override
public String getStars(String title) {

  // using where clause
  String stars = getJdbcTemplate().
    queryForObject("select stars from MOVIES where title=?",
      new Object[]{title}, String.class);

  return stars;
}
```

Here, ideally the second argument is passed via method arguments.

There are plenty of `queryForXXX` methods defined on the `JdbcTemplate`, such as `queryForInt`, `queryForList`, `queryForMap`, and so on. Please refer to the Spring Framework's API to understand the workings of these various methods.

Returning domain objects

The previous queries returned a single piece of data, movie stars, as we have seen in that case.

How can we retrieve a single row, say a `Movie` object for a given an id? The `JdbcTemplate`'s `queryForObject` method comes handy for such requirement. One additional thing we need to do is to pass a `RowMapper` instance.

The JDBC API returns a `ResultSet`, and we need to map each and every column of data from the `ResultSet` onto our domain objects. The Spring framework eliminates this repetitious process by providing the `RowMapper` interface.

Simply put, `RowMapper` is an interface for mapping table rows to a domain object. It has one method called `mapRow` that should be implemented by the concrete classes.

What we need to do is implement this interface to map our table columns to a `Movie` object. Let's implement a row mapper for our `Movie` domain object—see the snippet here:

```
public class MovieRowMapper implements RowMapper {
  Movie movie = null;
  public Object mapRow(ResultSet rs, int rowNum) throws SQLException{
    movie = new Movie();
    // This is where we extract data
    // from ResultSet and set it on Movie object

    movie.setID(rs.getString("id"));
    movie.setTitle(rs.getString("title"));
    ...
    return movie;

  }
}
```

Basically, the idea is to extract the relevant columns from the `ResultSet` and populate our `Movie` domain object and return it.

Now that our `MovieRowMapper` is implemented, use `jdbcTemplate` to retrieve the results.

```
@Override
public Movie getMovie(String id){

  String sql = "select * from MOVIES where id=?";
```

```
    return getJdbcTemplate().queryForObject(sql,
      new Object[]{id},new MovieRowMapper());
}
```

The `JdbcTemplate` executes the query by binding the argument and invoking the `Mov ieRowMapper` with a returned `ResultSet` from the query.

We need to enhance this logic a bit more to get *all* the movies (as a list) instead of a single movie result.

We can use the same `MovieRowMapper` for returning all the movies. However, it should be wrapped in a `RowMapperResultSetExtractor` as shown here:

```
public List getAllMovies(){
  RowMapper mapper = new MovieRowMapper();
  String sql = "select * from MOVIES";

  return getJdbcTemplate().query(sql,
    new RowMapperResultSetExtractor(mapper,10));
}
```

Manipulating data

We can use the `jdbcTemplate.update()` method to insert, update, or delete the data. The following code shows the insertion of `Movie` into our database.

```
@Override
public void insertMovie(Movie m) {
  String sql = "insert into MOVIES (ID, TITLE, GENRE, SYNOPSIS)
    values(?,?,?,?)";

  // The insert parameters
  Object[] params = new Object[] { m.getID(), m.getTitle(), m.getGenre(),
m.getSynopsis() };

  // The insert parameters types
  int[] types = new int[] { Types.VARCHAR, Types.VARCHAR, Types.VARCHAR,
Types.VARCHAR };

  // Run the query
  jdbcTemplate.update(sql, params, types);
}
```

The second and third parameters indicate the input values and their respective types.

Similarly, deleting a single movie from the database is straightforward:

```
@Override
public void deleteMovie(String id) {
  String sql = "delete from MOVIES where ID=?";
  Object[] params = new Object[] { id };
  jdbcTemplate.update(sql, params);
}
```

In order to delete all movies, use the following code:

```
@Override
public void deleteAllMovies(){
  String sql = "delete from MOVIES";
  jdbcTemplate.update(sql);
}
```

Calling stored procedures is also an easy thing, using the update method:

```
public void deleteAllMovies(){
  String sql = "call MOVIES.DELETE_ALL_MOVIES";
  jdbcTemplate.update(sql);
}
```

As we have noticed, the JdbcTemplate has eased our burden in accessing the database dramatically. I advise you to refer to Spring's API for more such methods on the template class.

Hibernate

Hibernate provides a mapping of database columns to the objects by reading some configurations. We define the mapping of our domain objects to the table columns in the XML configuration file.

The configuration file for each of the mappings should have an extension of *.hbm.xml*. Spring abstracts the framework one step more and provides us with classes like Hiber nateTemplate to access the database. However, Spring advocates to drop Hibernate Template in favour of using Hibernate's native API.

We'll look into details in a minute, but first let's see how we can prepare the required configurations.

For example, let's define our MOVIE object by using hibernate mapping rules.

```
<hibernate-mapping>
  <class name="com.madhusudhan.jscore.data.Movie" table="MOVIES">
  <id name="id" column="ID">
    <generator class="assigned"/>
  </id>
  <property name="title" column="TITLE"/>
  <property name="genre" column="GENRE"/>
  <property name="synopsis" column="SYNOPSIS"/>
  </class>
</hibernate-mapping>
```

The class attribute defines the actual domain class, Movie in this case. The id attribute is the primary key and is set as assigned, meaning it is the application's responsibility to set the primary key. The rest of the properties are mapped against the respective columns on the MOVIES table.

Hibernate requires a Session object in order to access the database. A Session is created from the SessionFactory. When using Spring framework, you can use Spring's LocalSessionFactoryBean to create this SessionFactory. The LocalSessionFactoryBean requires a datasource to be wired in, along with hibernate properties and mapping resources.

The hibernateProperties attribute on the factory bean enables the database specific properties such as database dialect, pool sizes, and other options. The mappingResources property loads the mapping config files (*Movie.hbm.xml*, in our case).

```xml
<bean id="sessionFactory"
  class="org.springframework.orm.hibernate.LocalSessionFactoryBean">
  <property name="dataSource" ref="movieDataSource" />
  <property name="hibernateProperties">
    <props>
      <prop key="hibernate.dialect">net.sf.hibernate.dialect.MySQLDialect</prop>
      <prop key="hibernate.show_sql">false</prop>
    </props>
  </property>
  <property name="mappingResources">
    <list>
      <value>Movie.hbm.xml</value>
    </list>
  </property>
</bean>
```

Using old style HibernateTemplate

Now that the sessionFactory is defined, the next bit is to define HibernateTemplate. The HibernateTemplate requires a SessionFactory instance, so the following declaration wires the sessionFactory that we defined above.

```xml
<bean id="hibernateTemplate"
  class="org.springframework.orm.hibernate.HibernateTemplate">
    <property name="sessionFactory" ref="sessionFactory"/>
</bean>

<bean id="movieDao"
  class="com.madhusudhan.jscore.data.MovieDAO">
  <property name="hibernateTemplate" ref="hibernateTemplate"/>
</bean>
```

That's all—the configuration is completed. Let's see how we get the data from our database.

The getMovie method shown here uses the template's load method.

```java
public Movie getMovie(String id){
  //Searching for a movie
  return (Movie)getHibernateTemplate().load (Movie.class, id);
}
```

As you can see, there's no SQL that retrieves a movie in this method. It feels like we are working with Java objects rather than data! The load method accesses the database to load the matching row based on the id passed.

Updating a Movie is simple as well:

```
public void updateMovie(Movie m){
   //Updating a movie
   getHibernateTemplate().update (m);
}
```

As you can see, the single statement above does the job! Deleting a row is as simple as invoking the delete method.

```
public void deleteMovie(Movie m){
   // Deleting a movie
   getHibernateTemplate().delete (m);
}
```

Running queries is straightforward, too. Hibernate introduces Hibernate Query Language (HQL) for writing queries. Use find methods to execute such queries.

For example, returning a Movie based on a ID is shown here:

```
public Movie getMovie(String id){
   String sql="from MOVIES as movies where movies.id=?";
   // Finding a movie
   return (Movie)getHibernateTemplate().find(sql, id);
}
```

That's about using Hibernate from a very high ground. I strongly advise you to pick up any Hibernate book to understand in detail.

Preferred style—using native API

The recomended way to use Spring with Hibernate is to use Hibernate's API rather than Spring's template wrapper. The subject is provided at length in my other book *Just Spring Data Access*, so please go through it if you have the copy. For completness, let's browse through this style quickly.

The Hibernates's org.hibernate.SessionFactory and org.hibernate.Session forms the central part of the Hibernate API.

Spring provides a org.springframework.orm.hibernate3.LocalSessionFactory Bean to create a wrapper around the SessionFactory. This wrapper is then injected into our DAO object.

As expected, this bean should be wired in with a DataSource, along with other Hibernate properties. The configuration is almost same as the one shown earlier:

```
<bean id="sessionFactory"
   class="org.springframework.orm.hibernate3.LocalSessionFactoryBean">
```

```
    <property name="dataSource" ref="mySqlDataSource" />
    <property name="mappingResources">
      <list>
        <value>Trade.hbm.xml</value>
      </list>
    </property>
  <property name="hibernateProperties">
    <props>
     <prop key="hibernate.show_sql">false</prop>
     <prop key="hibernate.hbm2ddl.auto">true</prop>
     ....
    </props>
  </bean>
```

The `TradeDAO`, along with the injected SessionFactory, is declared here:

```
public class TradeDAO {
  private SessionFactory sessionFactory = null;
  public SessionFactory getSessionFactory() {
   return sessionFactory;
  }
  public void setSessionFactory(SessionFactory sessionFactory) {
    this.sessionFactory = sessionFactory;
  }
}
```

Once we have the handle to the `SessionFactory`, we can fetch a `Session` out of it by using `getSessionFactory().getCurrentSession()` method invocation. The session is the main interface that we should be using to do the database operations. For example, in order to persist the Trade, all we need to do is to call a `save` method on this ses sion. This is shown here:

```
public void persist(Trade t) {
  session.beginTransaction();
  session.save(t);
  session.getTransaction().commit();
}
```

That's it, you are done with persisting the trade—no messy SQL or `ResultSets` or `RowMappers`!

Note that each of these database operation should be carried in a transaction, hence we are surrounding our code by beginning a transaction and commiting the same.

There are a plethora of operations that you could carry out on the Session object—refer to the API to get more insight.

Summary

In this chapter, we discussed Spring's support of JDBC and Hibernate. As we have seen in the examples, Spring has truly simplified our lives by providing a simple yet powerful API to work with. We can concentrate on the business logic rather than writing reams of repetitive code fragments.

About the Author

Madhusudhan Konda is an experienced Java consultant working in London, primarily with investment banks and financial organizations. Having worked in enterprise and core Java for last 12 years, his interests lie in distributed, multi-threaded, n-tier scalable, and extensible architectures. He is experienced in designing and developing high-frequency and low-latency application architectures. He enjoys writing technical papers and is interested in mentoring.

Colophon

The bird on the cover of *Just Spring* is a Treeswift of the genus *Hemiprocne*.

The cover image is from Cassell's *Natural History*. The cover font is Adobe ITC Garamond. The text font is Adobe Minion Pro; the heading font is Adobe Myriad Condensed; and the code font is Dalton Maag's Ubuntu Mono.

Have it your way.

Get even more for your money.

Join the O'Reilly Community, and register the O'Reilly books you own. It's free, and you'll get:

- $4.99 ebook upgrade offer
- 40% upgrade offer on O'Reilly print books
- Membership discounts on books and events
- Free lifetime updates to ebooks and videos
- Multiple ebook formats, DRM FREE
- Participation in the O'Reilly community
- Newsletters
- Account management
- 100% Satisfaction Guarantee

Signing up is easy:

1. **Go to: oreilly.com/go/register**
2. **Create an O'Reilly login.**
3. **Provide your address.**
4. **Register your books.**

Note: English-language books only

To order books online:
oreilly.com/store

For questions about products or an order:
orders@oreilly.com

To sign up to get topic-specific email announcements and/or news about upcoming books, conferences, special offers, and new technologies:
elists@oreilly.com

For technical questions about book content:
booktech@oreilly.com

To submit new book proposals to our editors:
proposals@oreilly.com

O'Reilly books are available in multiple DRM-free ebook formats. For more information:
oreilly.com/ebooks

O'REILLY®

Spreading the knowledge of innovators | oreilly.com

CPSIA information can be obtained at www.ICGtesting.com
Printed in the USA
BVOW000759280513

321777BV00014B/185/P